Table Of Contents-1

To the men in my life:
my father & my husband
I wish I could have introduced
you to each other.

Shhh!

You cannot tell me who to love
You cannot tell me how to love
Only my heart controls that
Not you, your God or your hatred

I am loved by wonder
I am loved by strength
I am loved by beauty
No one can deny me that, except me

Fear tells us to hide
Fear tells us to lie
We cannot fear
Fear is how you win
Fear makes losers of us all

Love is not limited by small minds
Love is given by large spirit
Learn to love large
Love all as you claim to love your God

Learn that Love is larger than any of us
Learn that Love is the way we will all win
Learn that Love should not be hoarded
It will grow exponentially once given
Until we save the world, by loving ourselves

perspectives

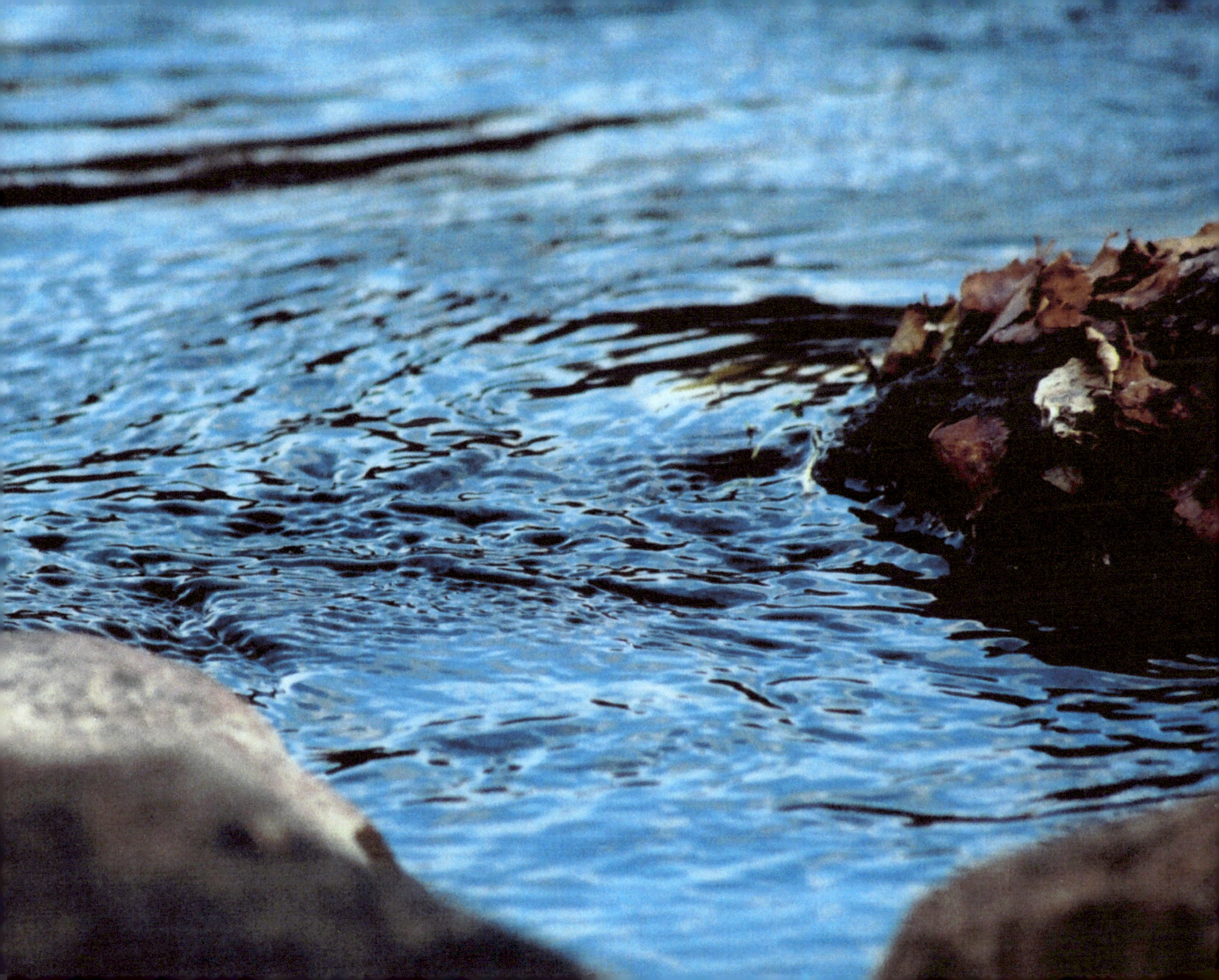

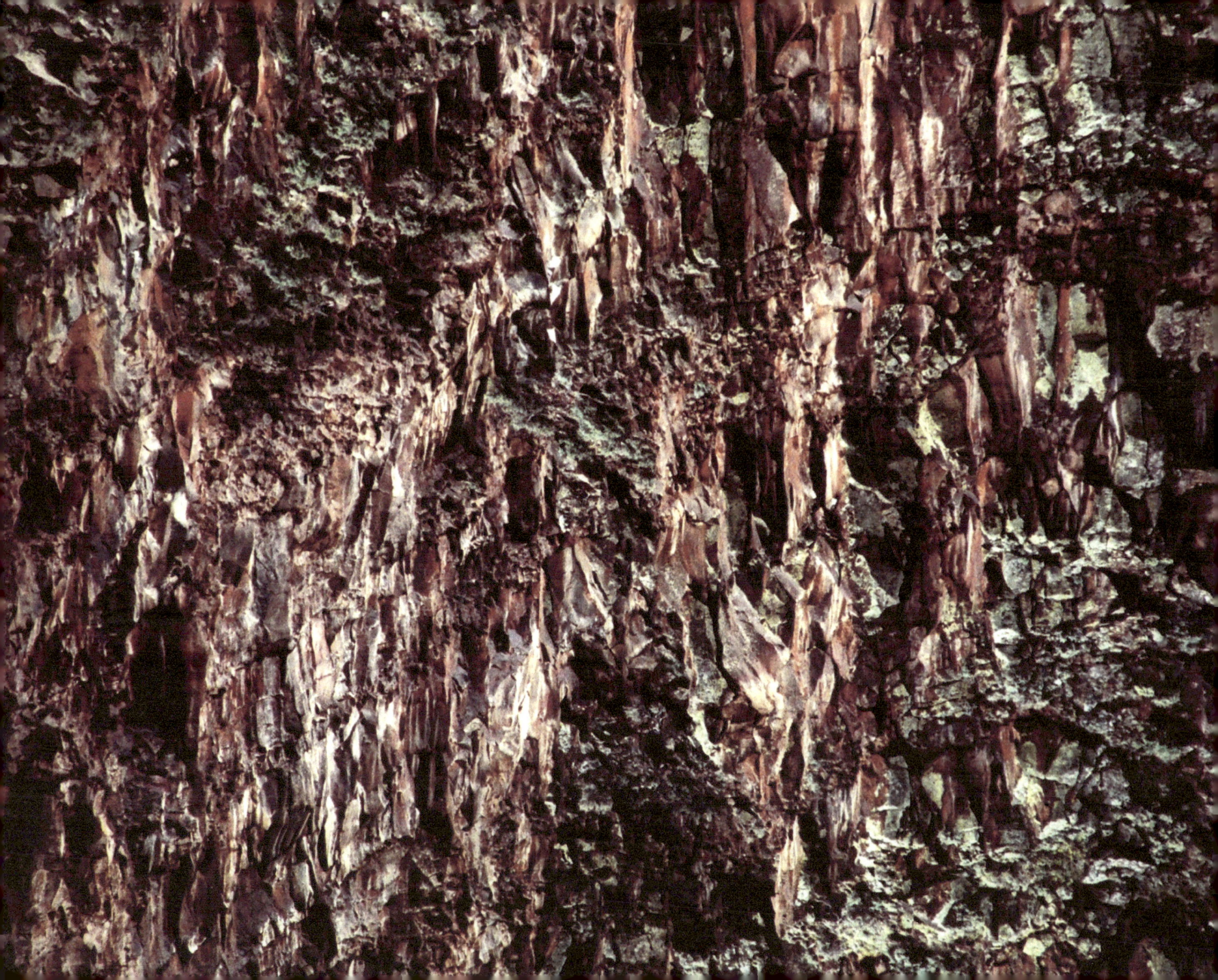

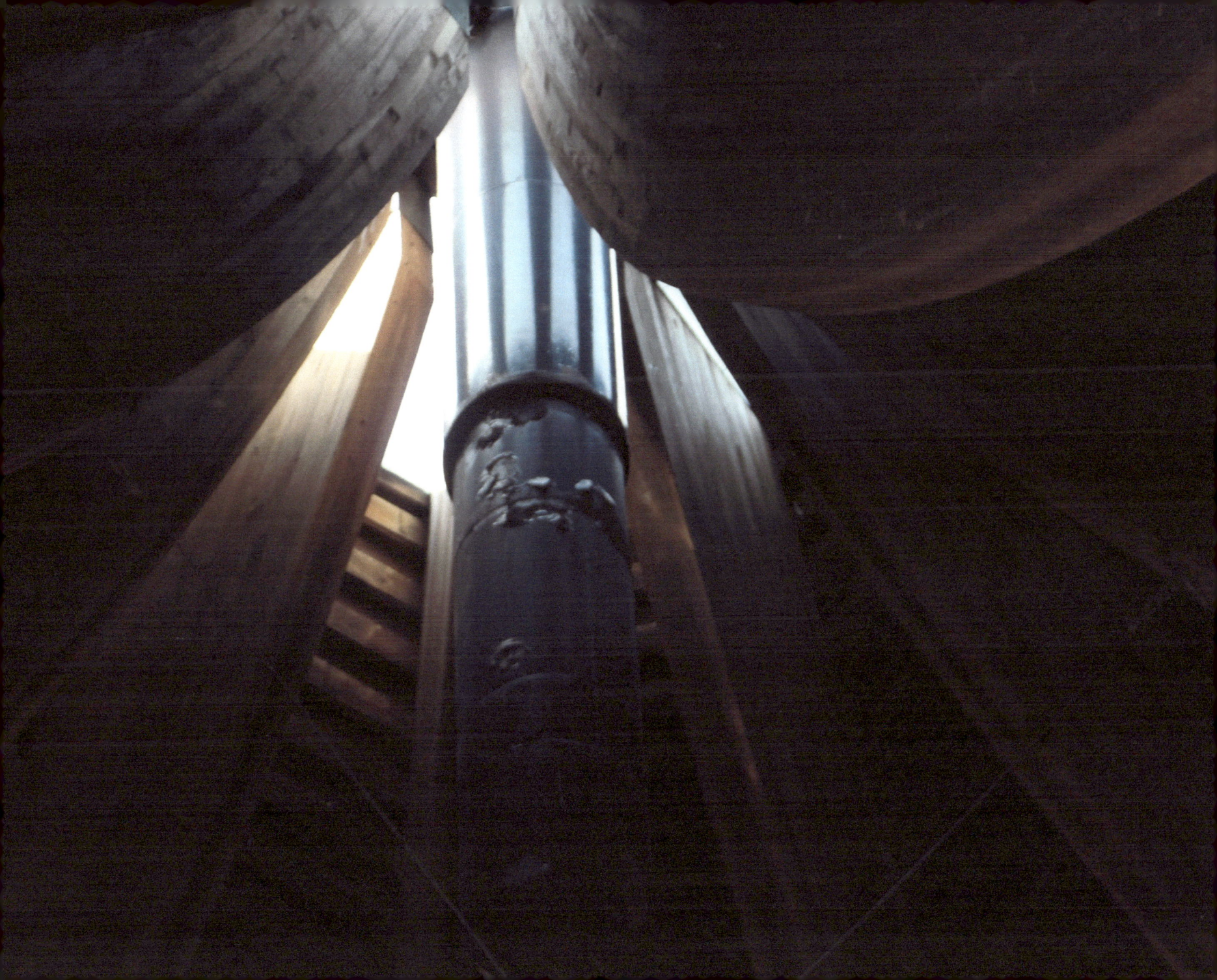

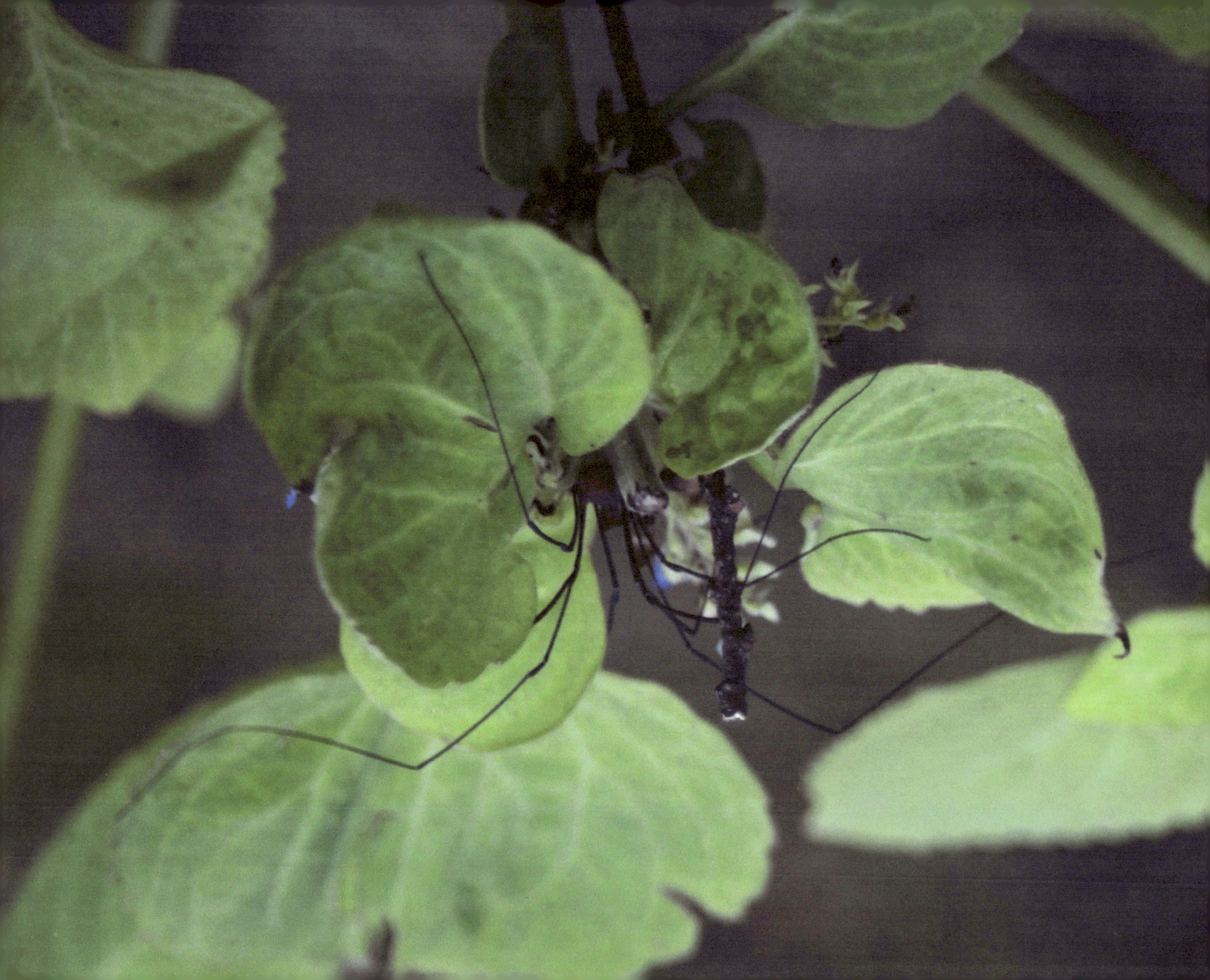

Your Business?

What I want
What I need
Who I love
Who I am
How I live
How I talk
Where I play
Where I laugh
Why I care
Why I write

What matters?
Who fears?
How said?
Where cautioned?
Why judge?

Ask
Learn
Know
Live

Color

#1

Why is nude a color?
Why is it not just an expression of who we are,
Skin tone holds no sin.
Be Proud of who and what you are.
Bathe in the beauty of you

#2

Why limit yourself to the colors of a rainbow?
Create Love and live outside the boundaries.
Let life be limitless and grow beyond your wildest dreams.

#3

All the shades of beautiful
How many crayons are in your box?
Where is your paper bag?
Do NOT limit your vision
Do NOT limit your choice.
Look at all of the shades
See all of the beauty

the american dream

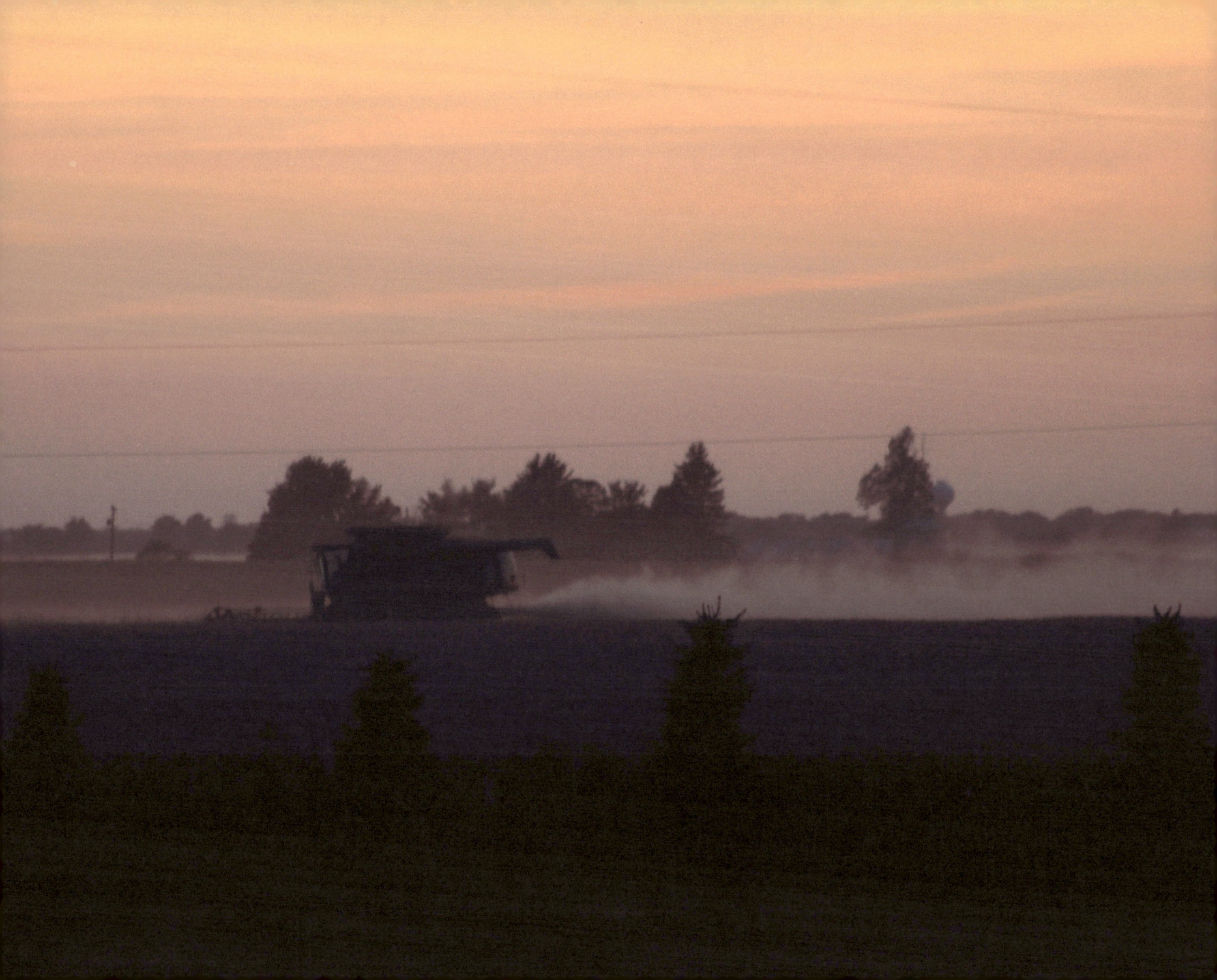

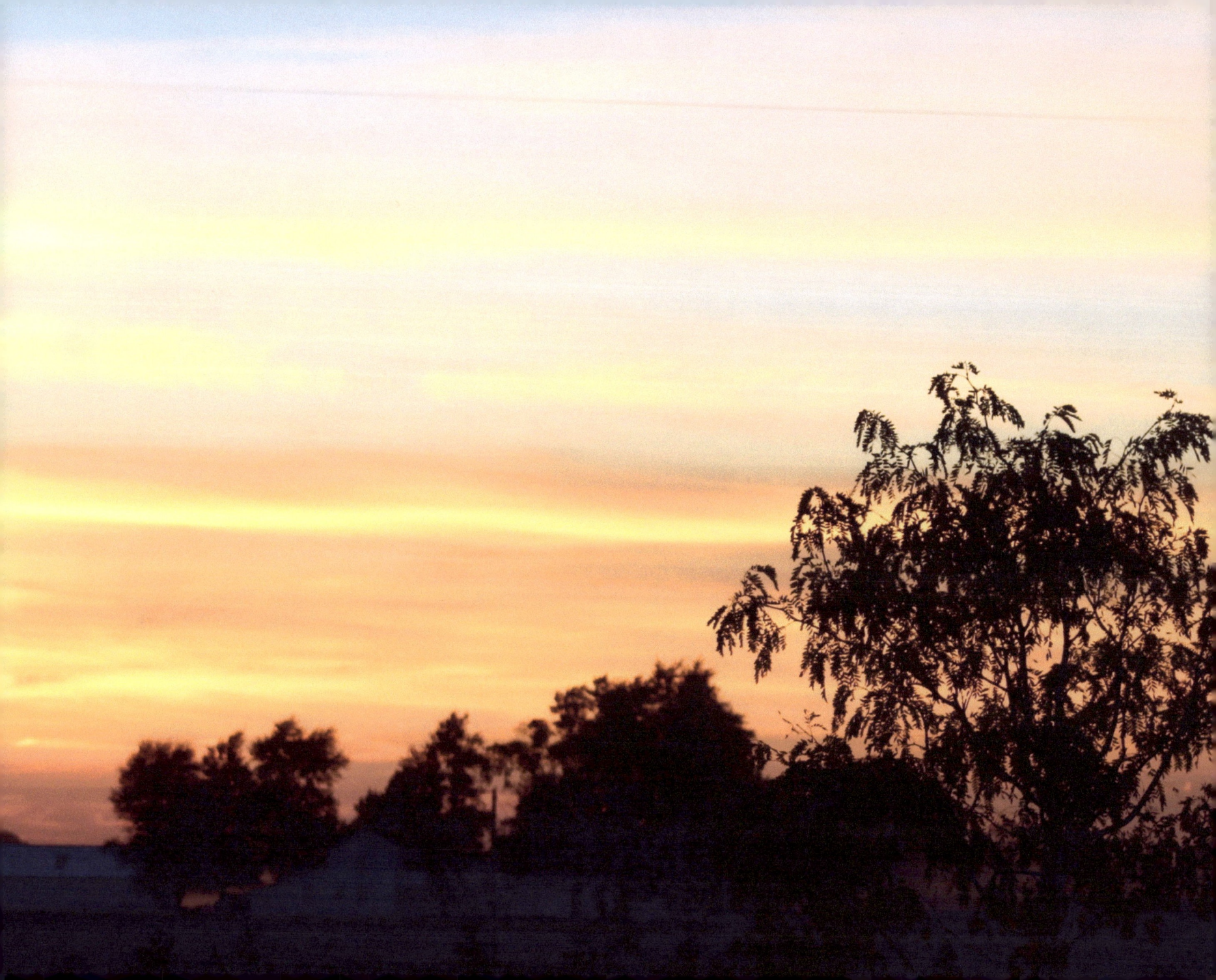

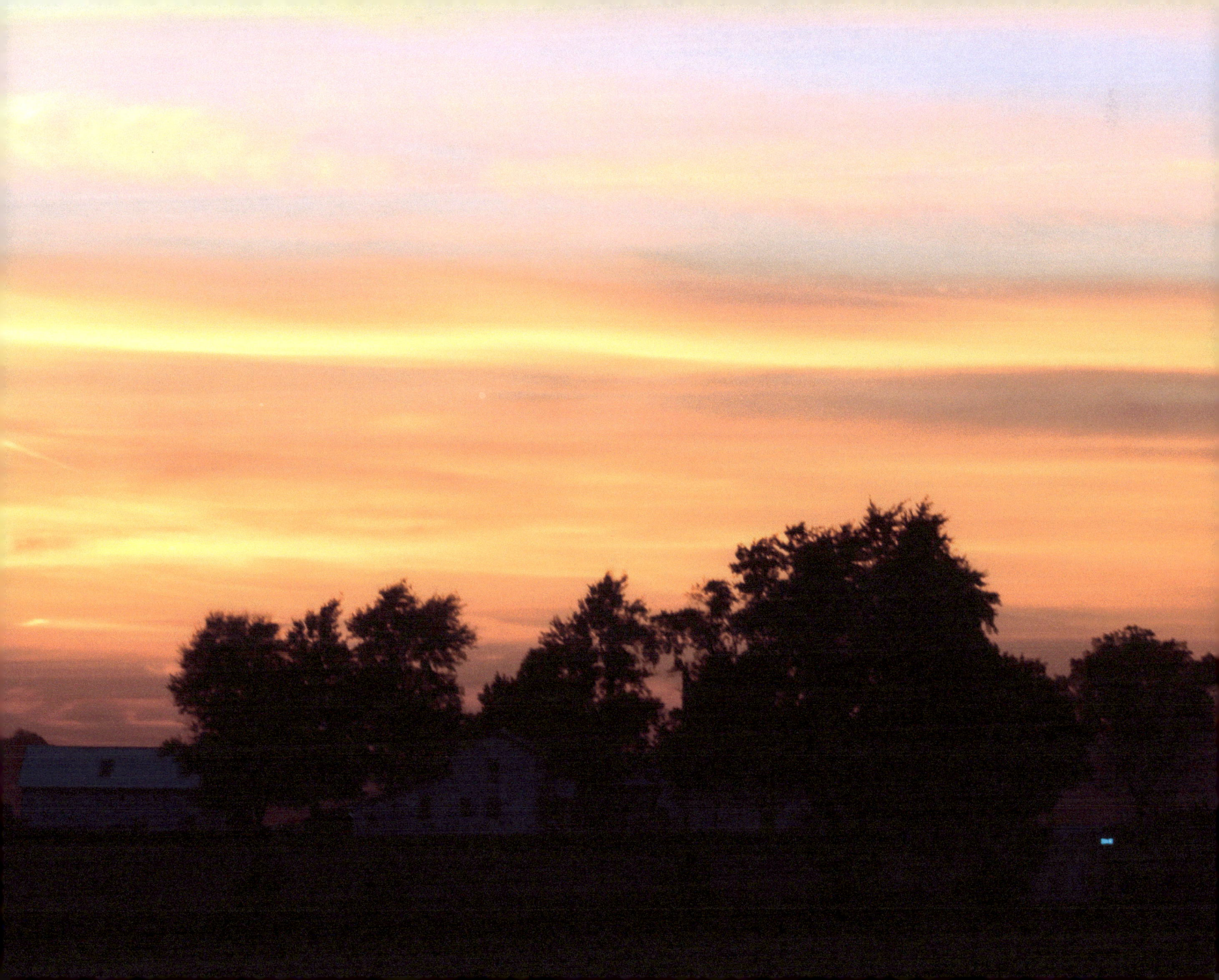

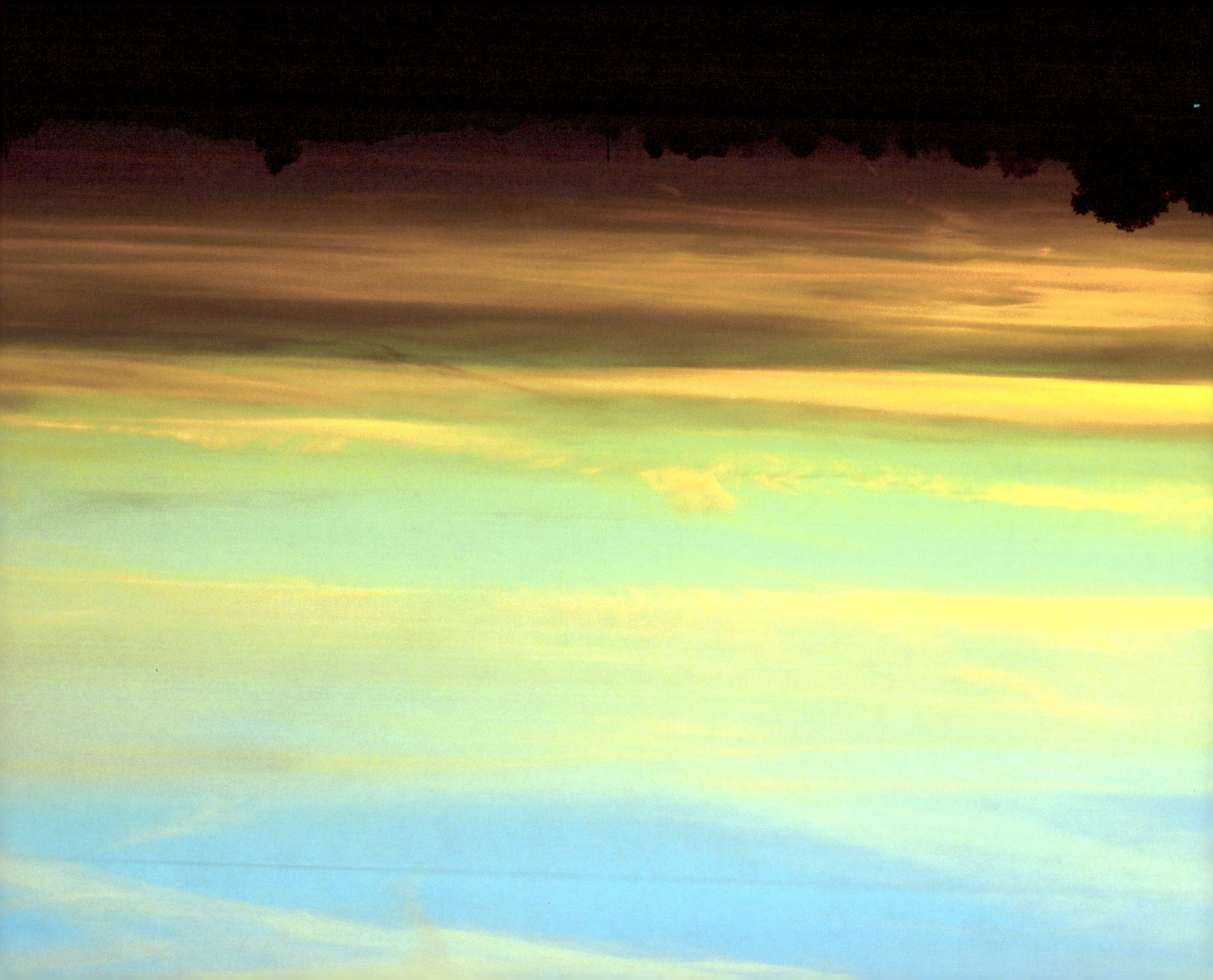

Secrets

There are things you cannot share
things you do not dare.
There are things that make you sad
when all you wish is to be mad.
There are things that stop you in your tracks
and make others turn their backs.
There are things you wouldn't show
that no one truly wants to know.

It's best if these things stay hidden away
forever and a day.
A promise broken, a promise kept
broken hearts under rugs, swept.
There are things I wish to say,
if only I could find a way.

sometimes it is black & white

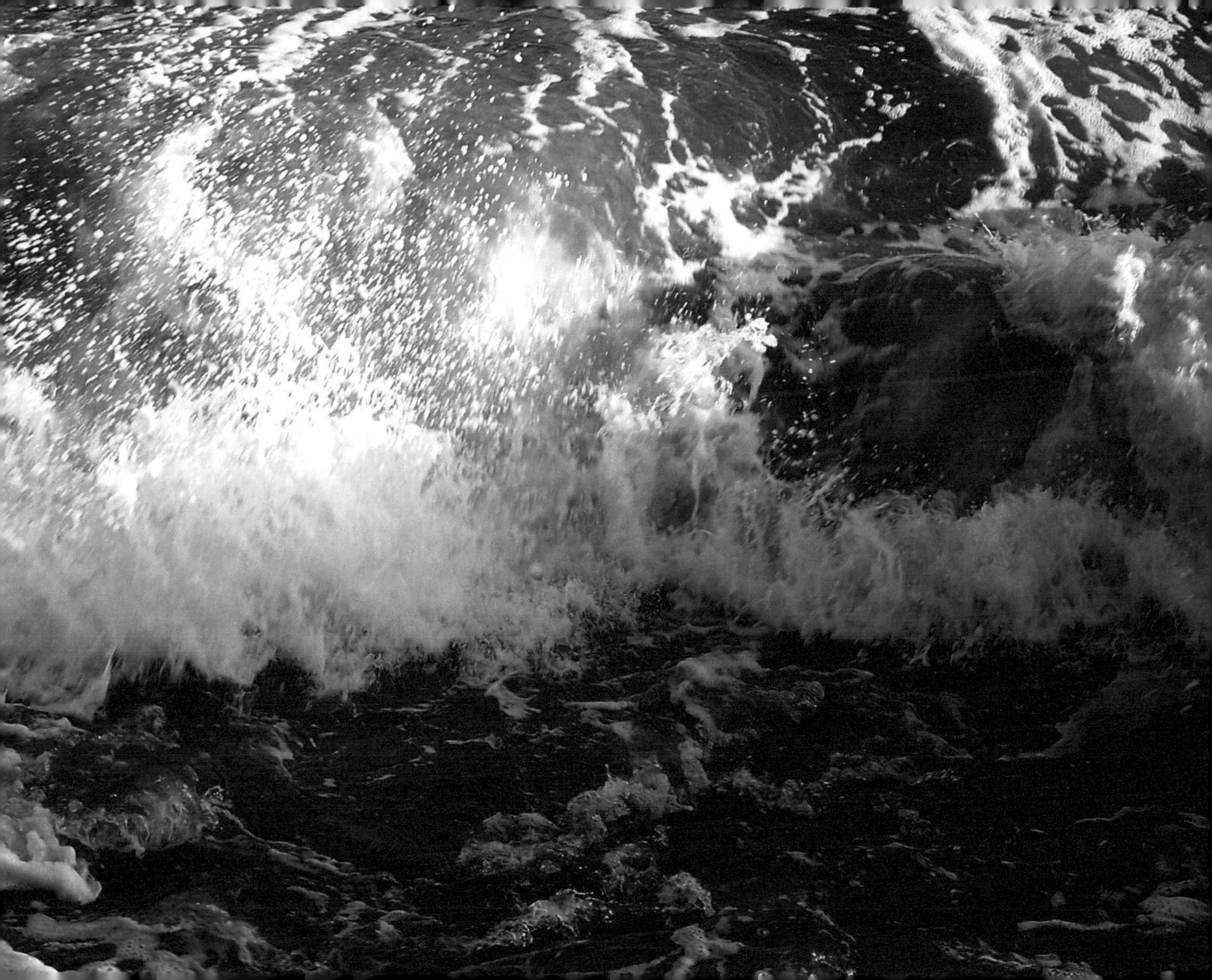

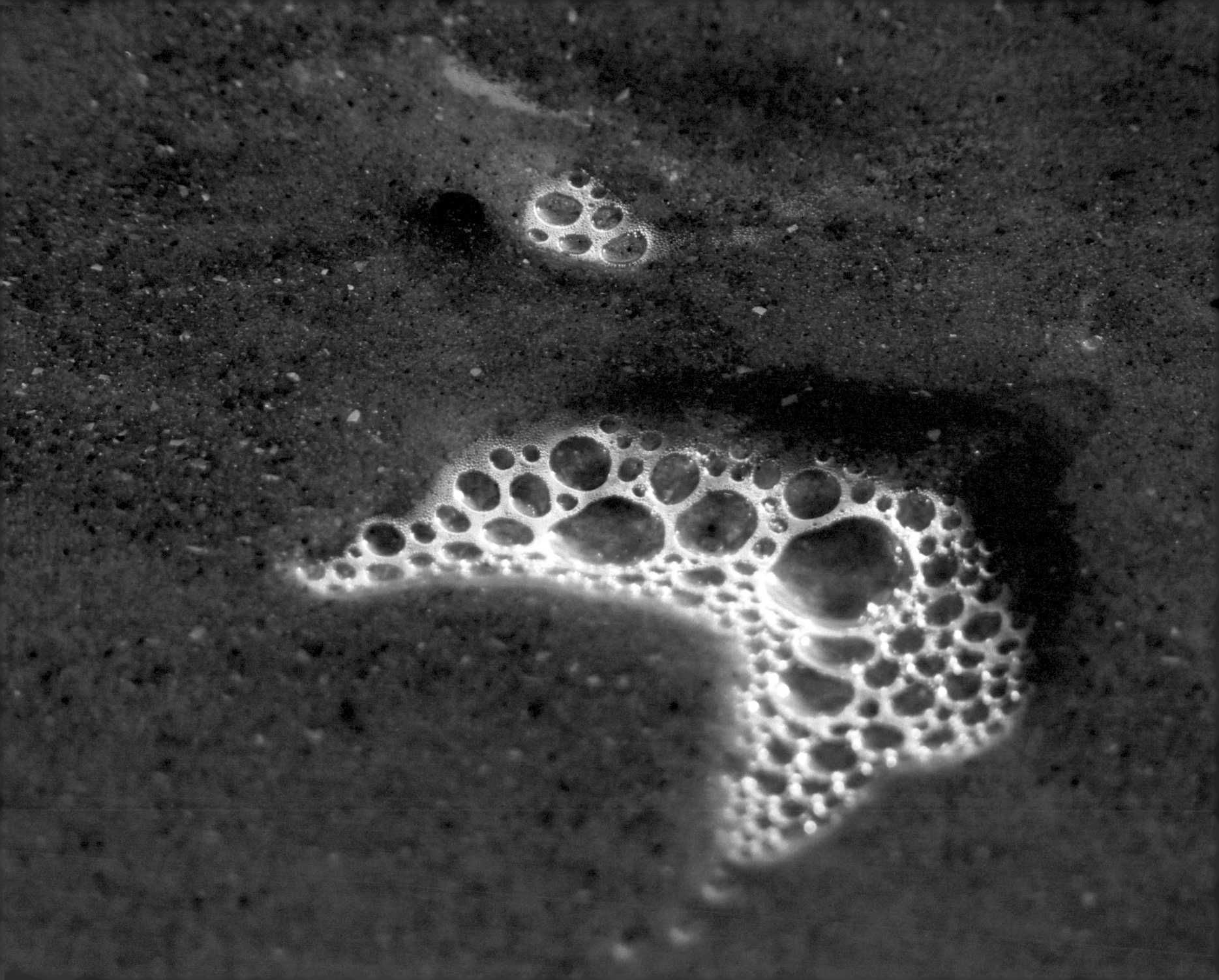

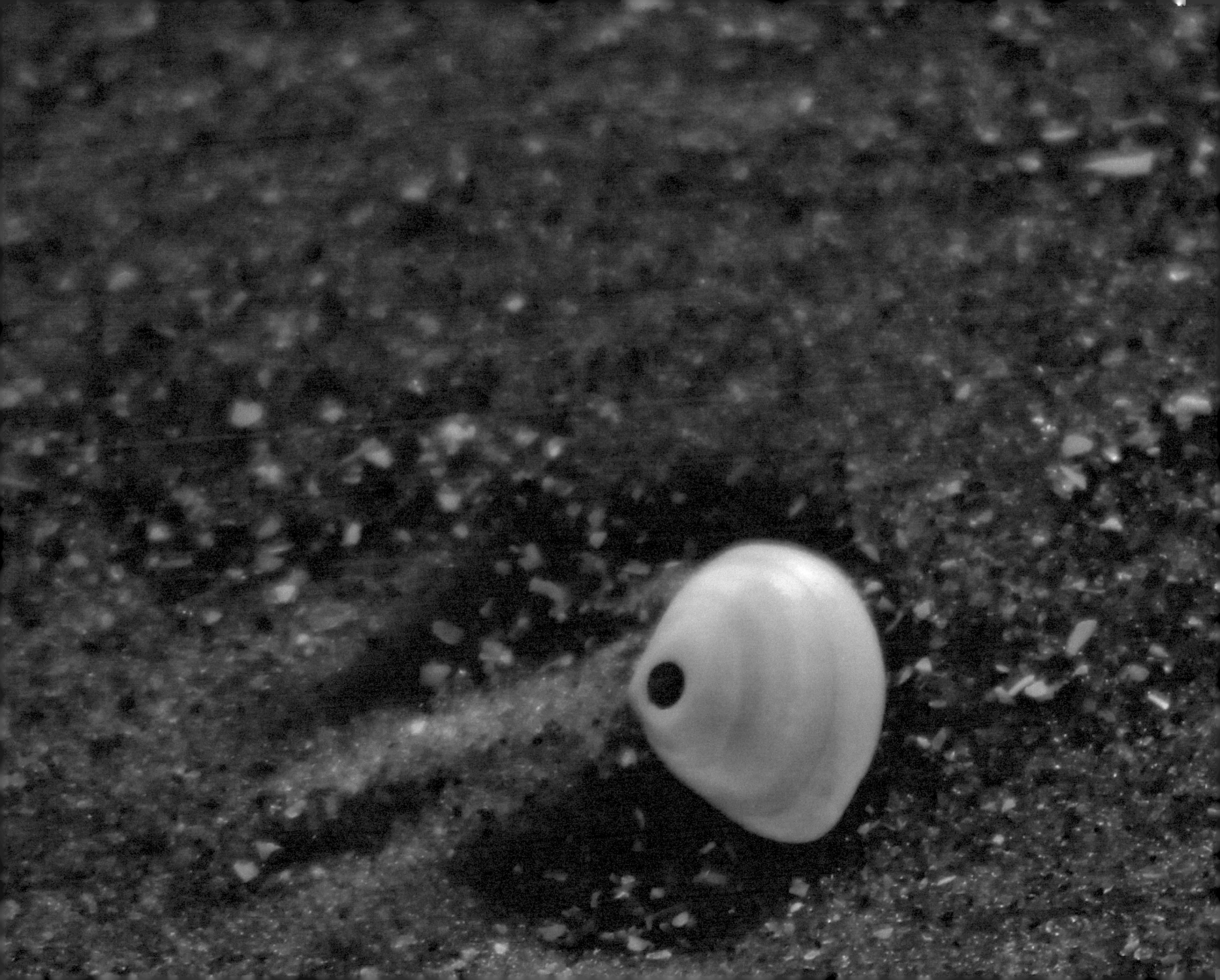

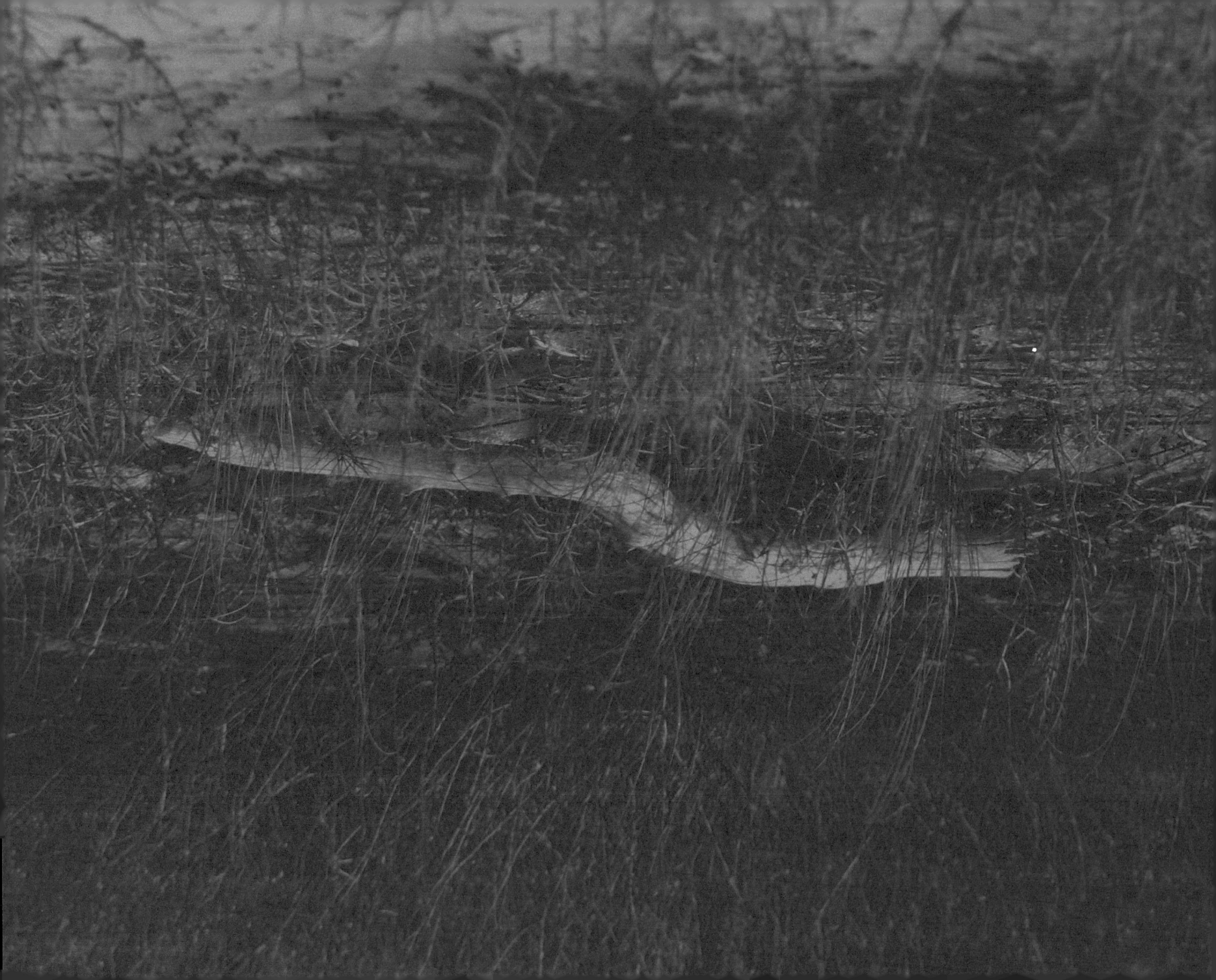

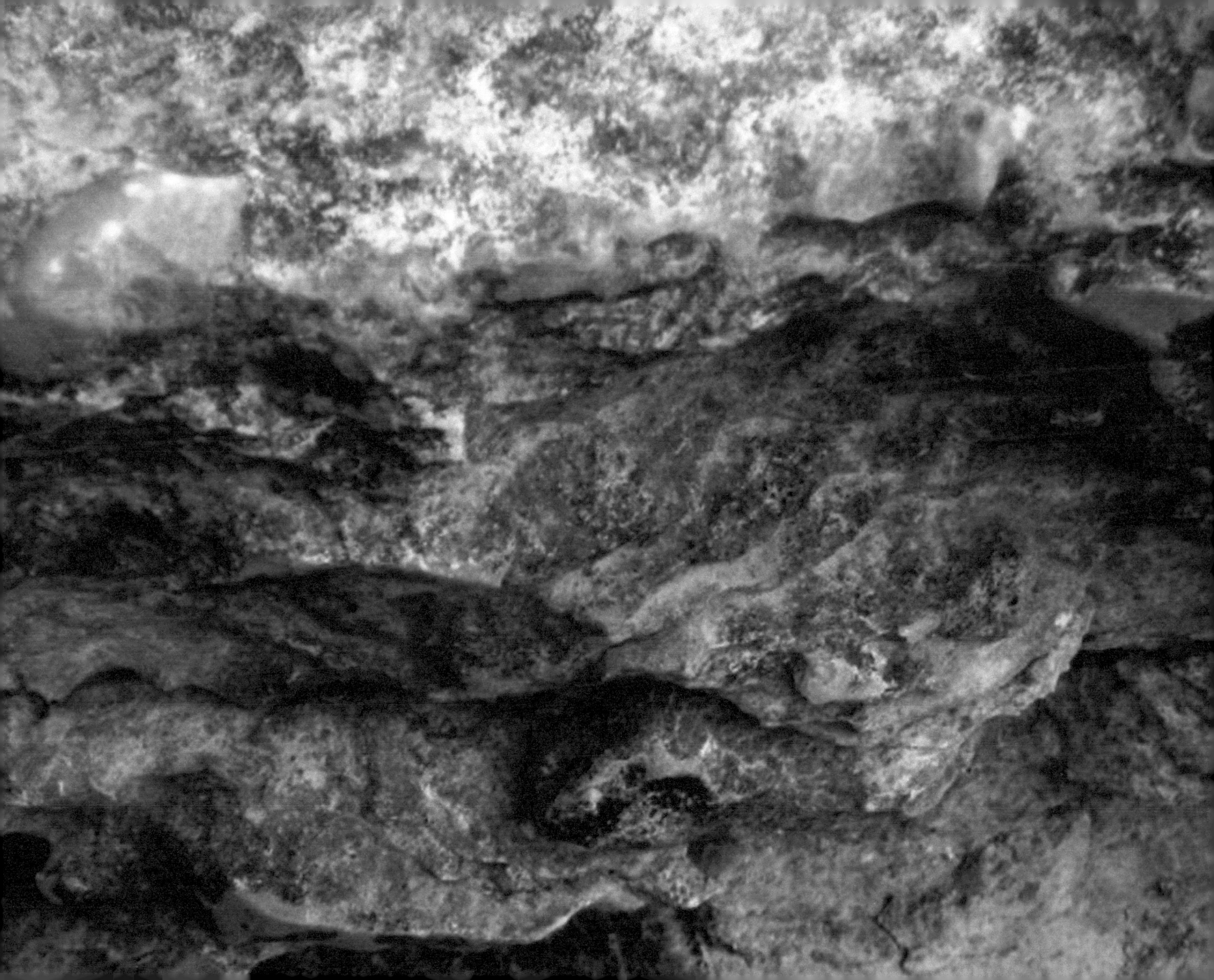

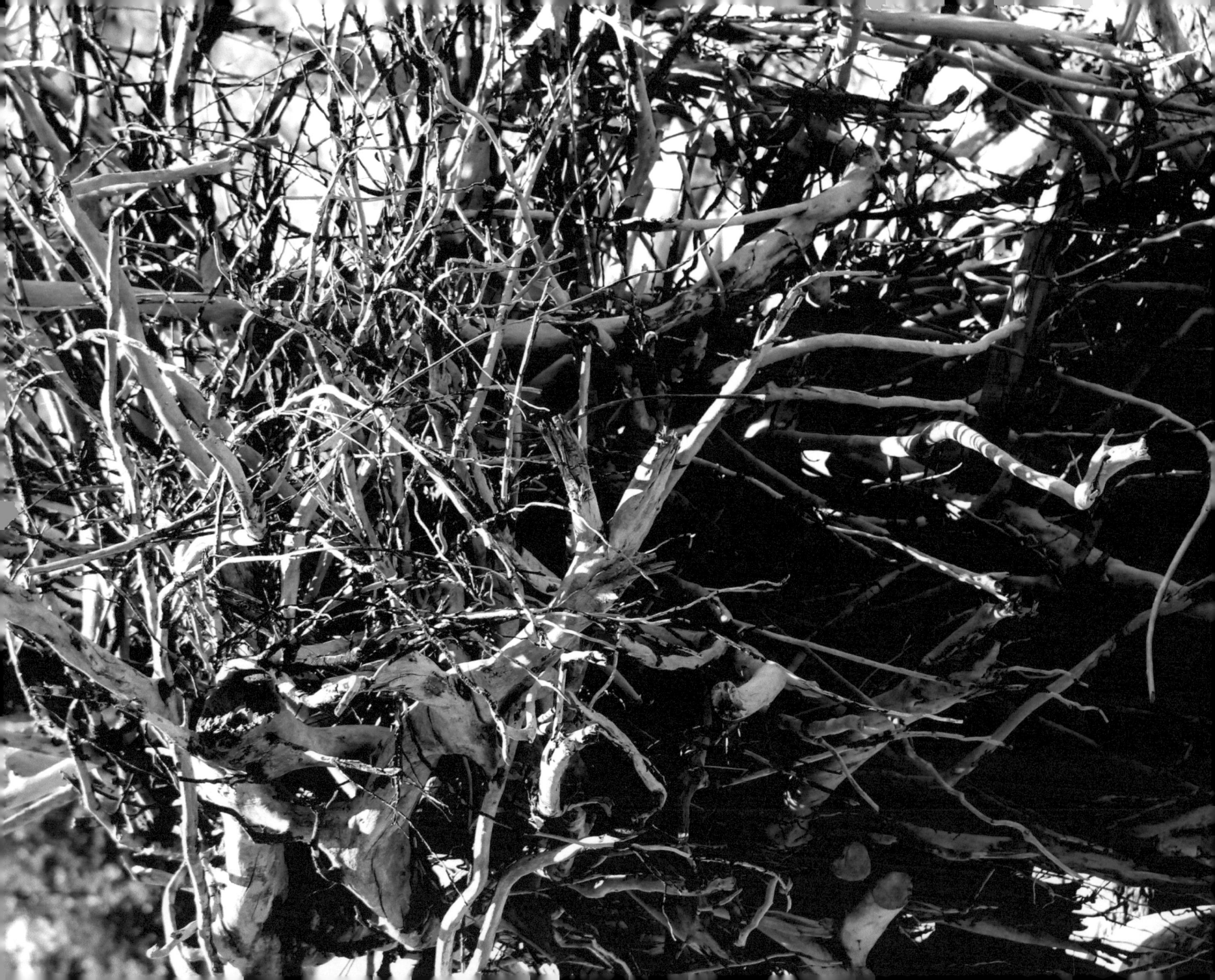

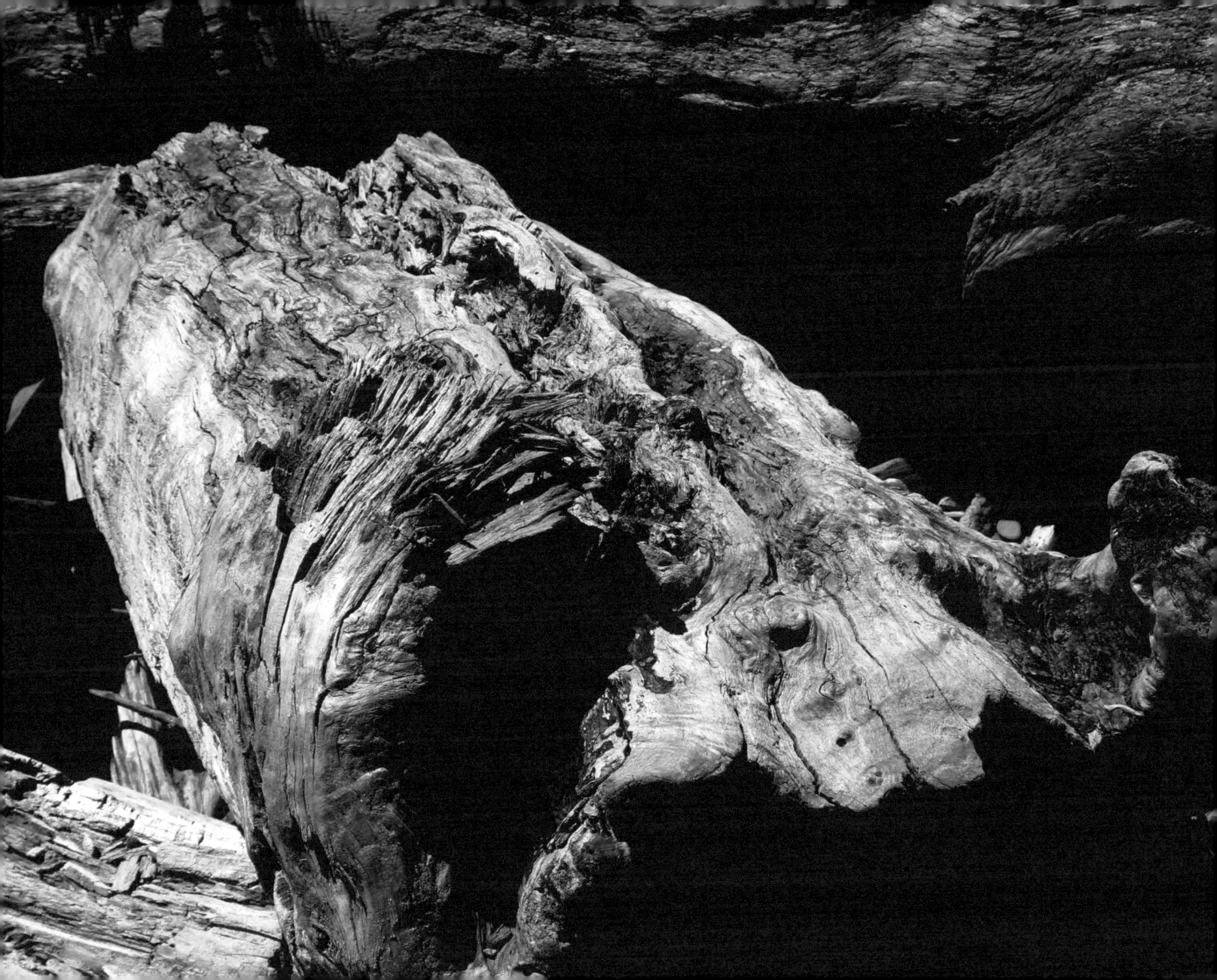

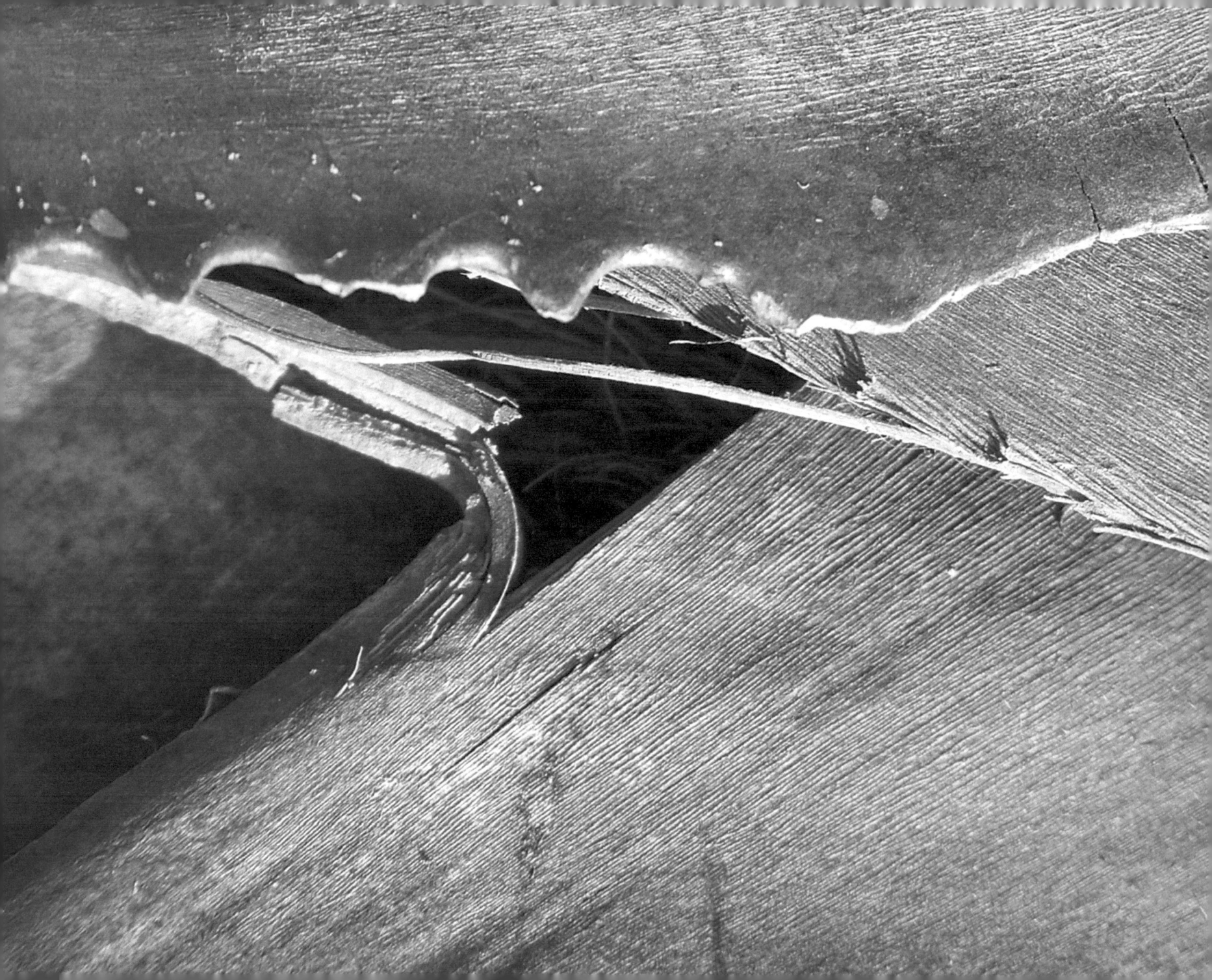

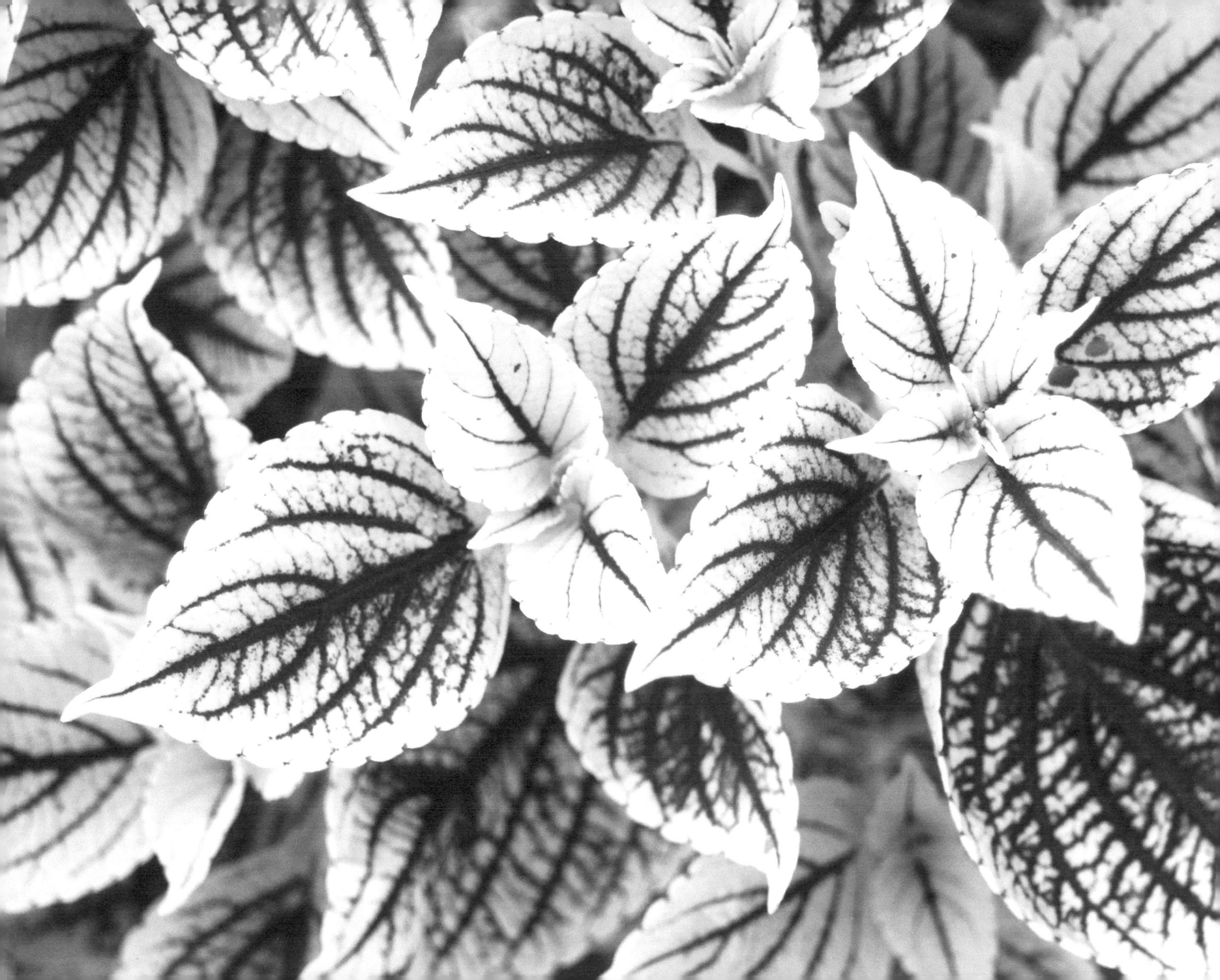

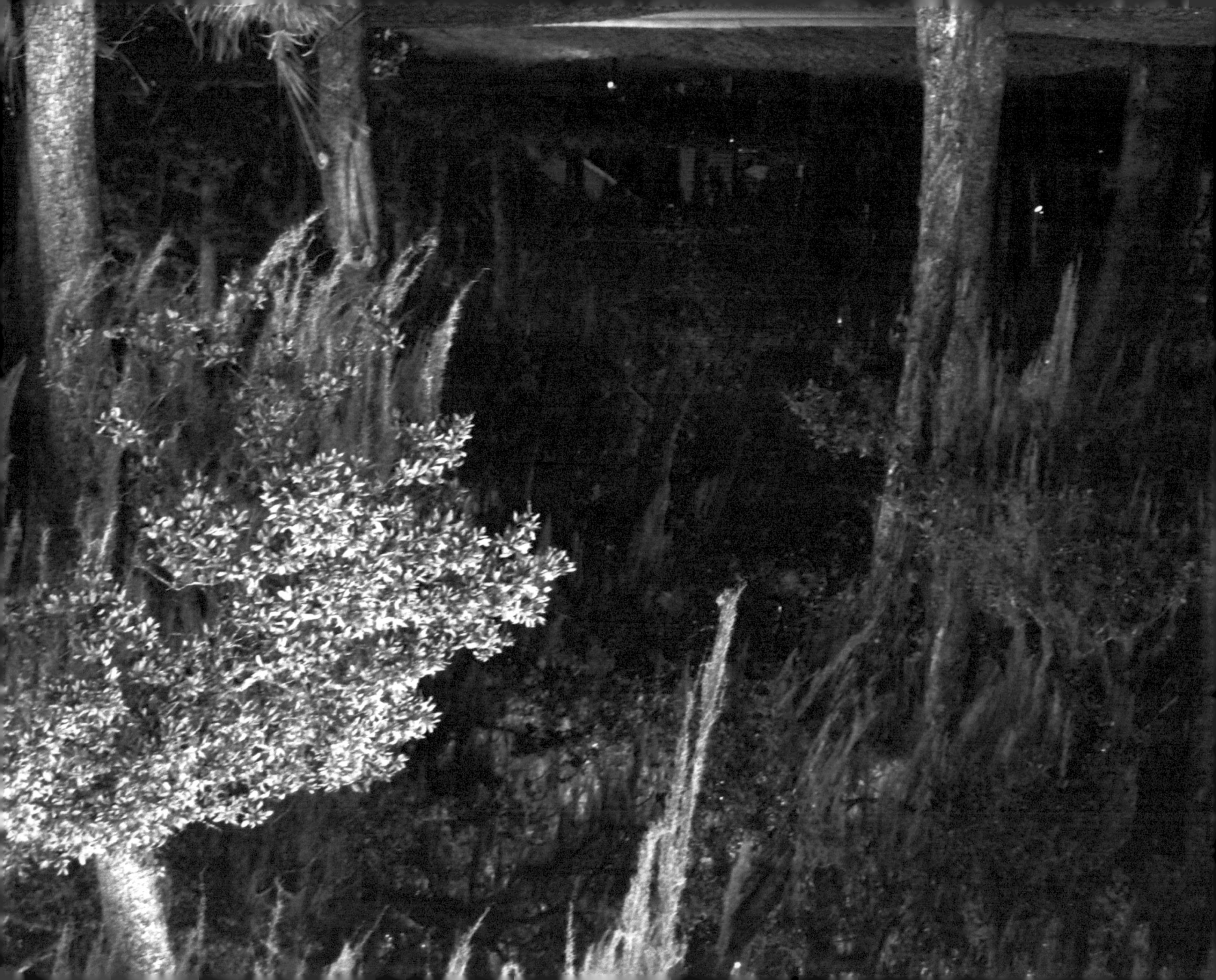

New Love

Every Night as I lie in your arms
Your breath touches my skin
Passion flows in my veins
Love lives in my heart and
Wonder lights in my head
For it is every night that I lie in your arms…

Home

Lands painted the colors of the rainbow
Cliffs formed by a greater hand
The land calls
Are we deaf?
Or have we chosen to ignore?
Shades of brown, red and gold
It is just dirt and sand
Or is it more?
Answer the call and feel…
Feel the wind on your face
The heat on your skin
The earth beneath you
And the sky above.
The touch of your gods
Welcoming you home.

Scars

Living easy isn't living
Going with the flow
From one day to the next
Means being just like everyone else
Life is hard
It is supposed to be
Easy Lessons are learned easily
The hard ones are supposed to hurt
So you can point at the scar
And say it was worth it.
Live life HARD and live life.

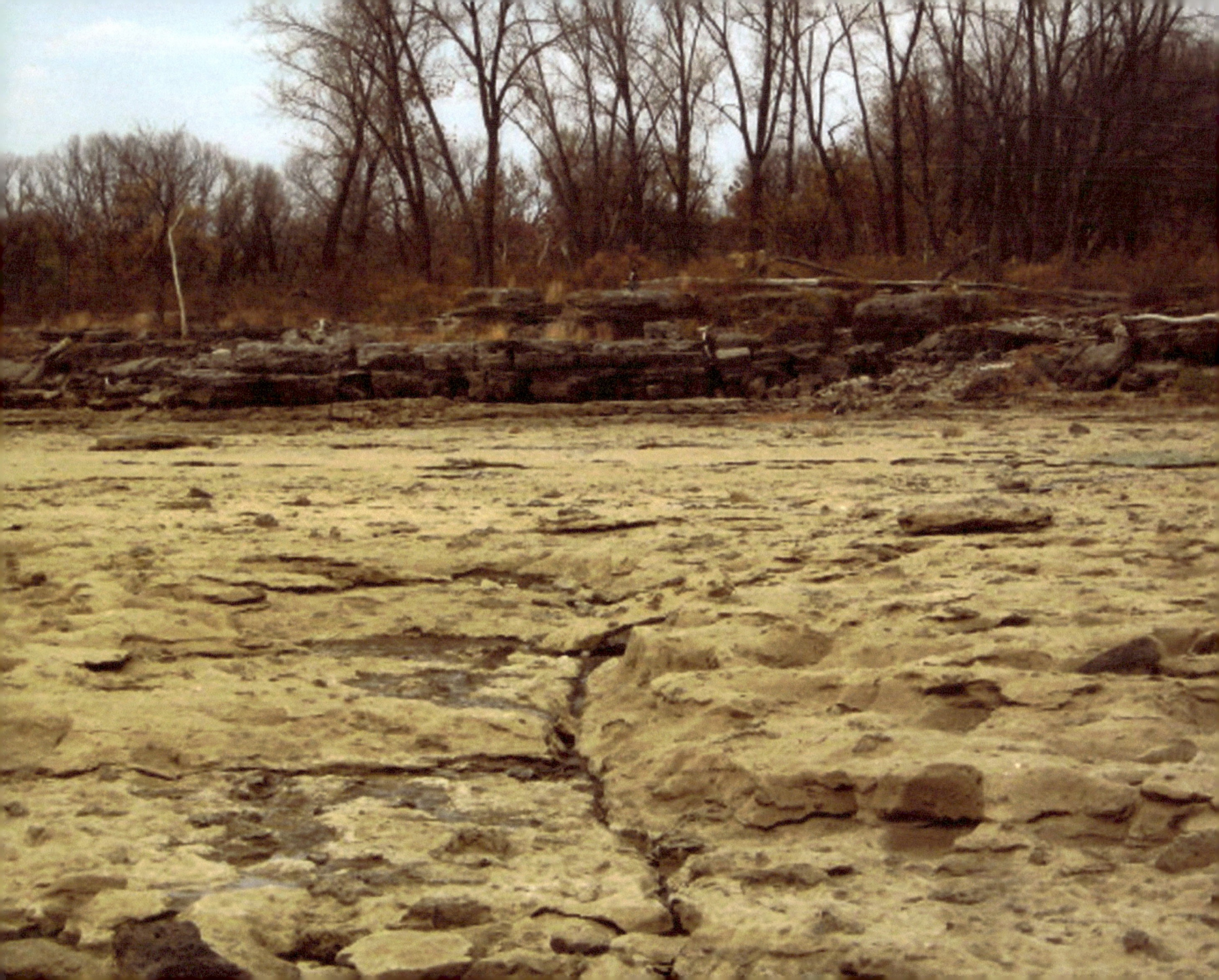

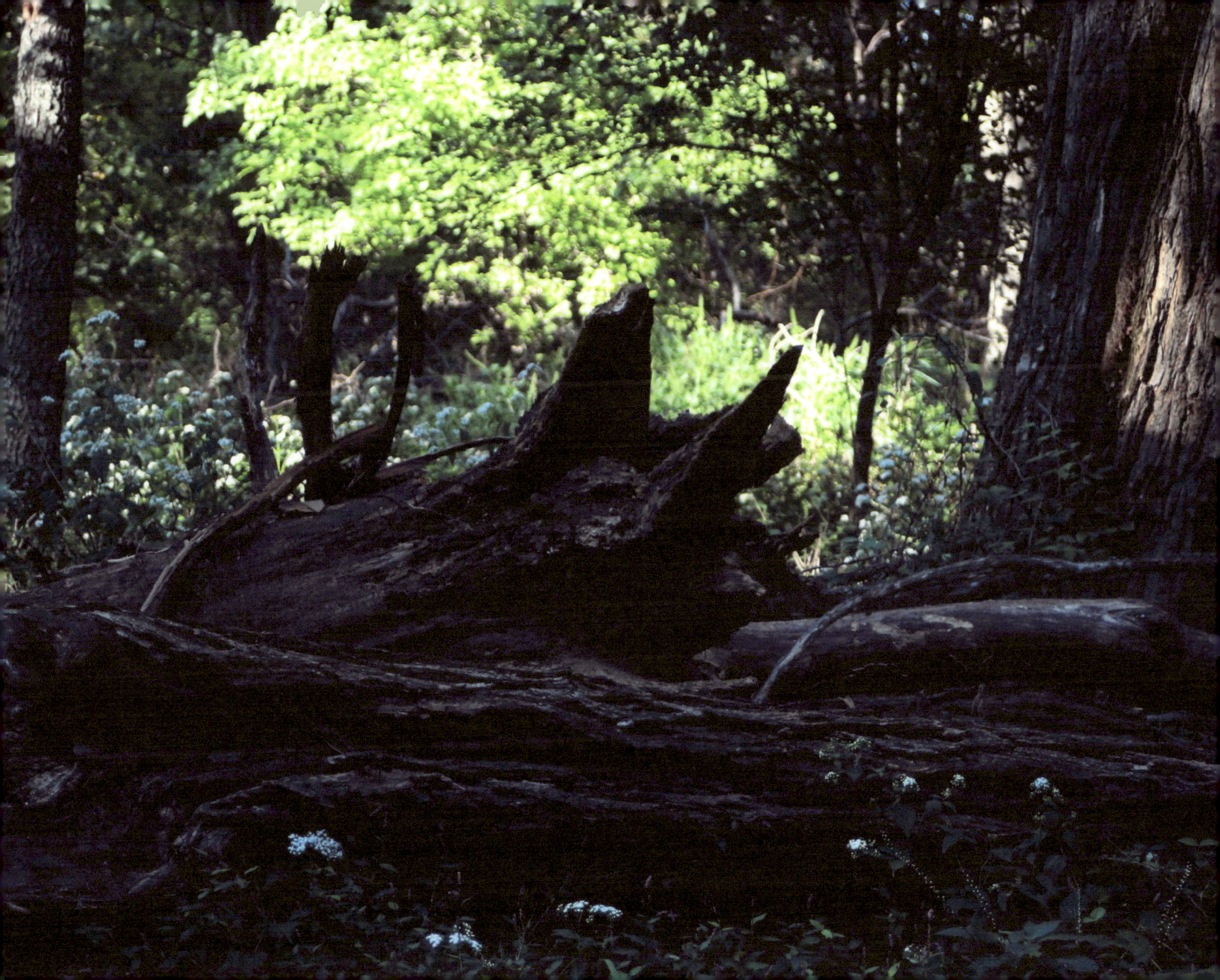

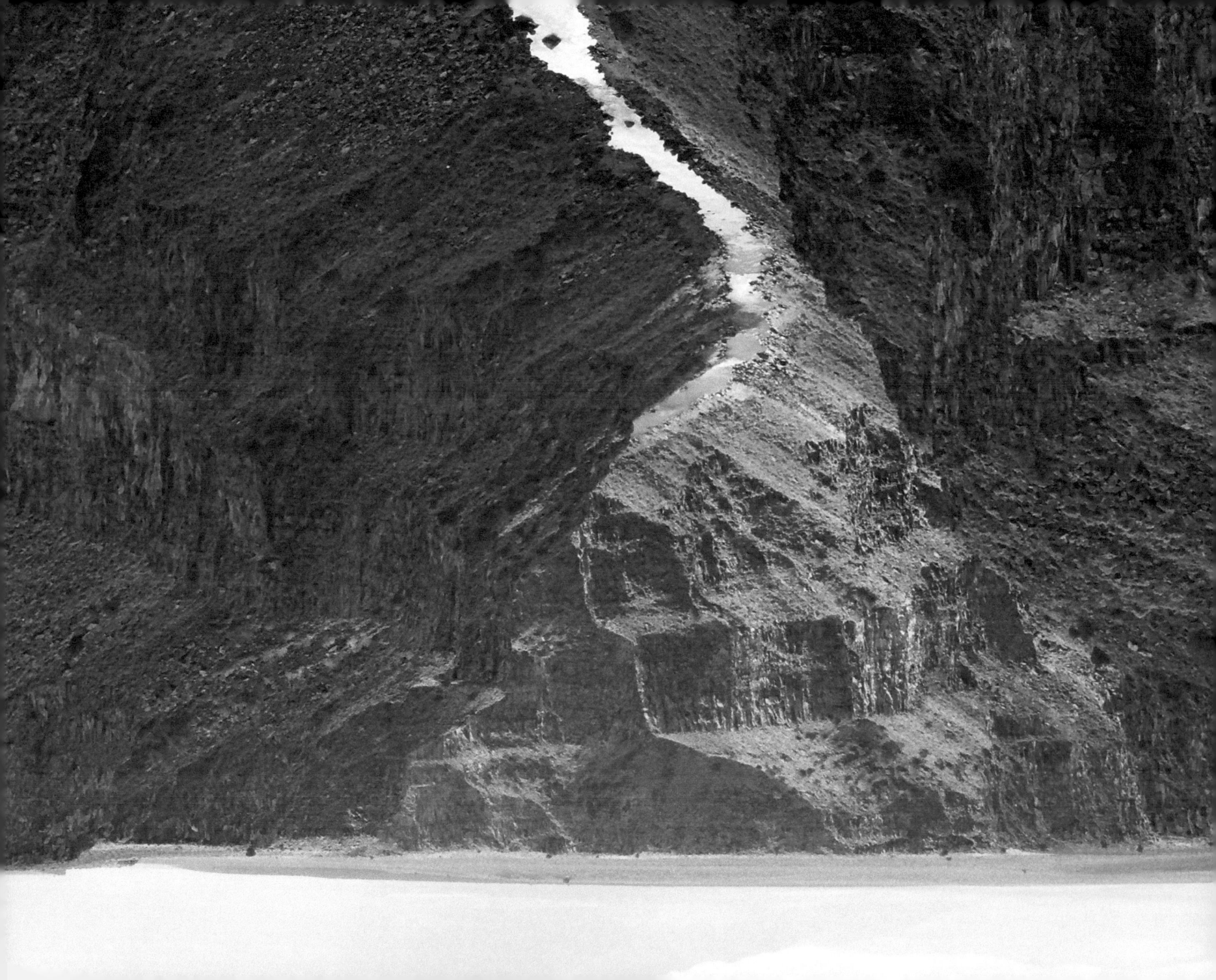

Grief

#1
My heart hurts.
My stomach turns.
My tears fall.
I miss you.
You were my rock.
You were our shelter.
You are Dad…
And you are gone.
I remember
And I weep
I ache
And I burn.
I know you walk beside me.
I wish I could feel your hug.
You would love them too.
It's what makes me so very sad.
Tomorrow is forever
Today will go away
The past is a fading memory.
Stay in my heart
Know my dreams
See my joys
Feel my sorrows.
Kiss my hurts
Heal my wounds
Patch the scrapes
I miss you
I love you
I need you
Father

#2
I am not a mother
Yet I am their Mom, their grandma and
I was his Great Grandmother
We only met twice,
Yet he was my baby
Blood is not the only connection
Family is of the soul
He will be missed
Another piece of my heart taken early

#3
The Mother cries
For the life She had to take
For the hearts She had to break
Not because it was his time
Not because it was our time
But because it was Her time
So gently She weeps
As the tears roll down our cheeks.

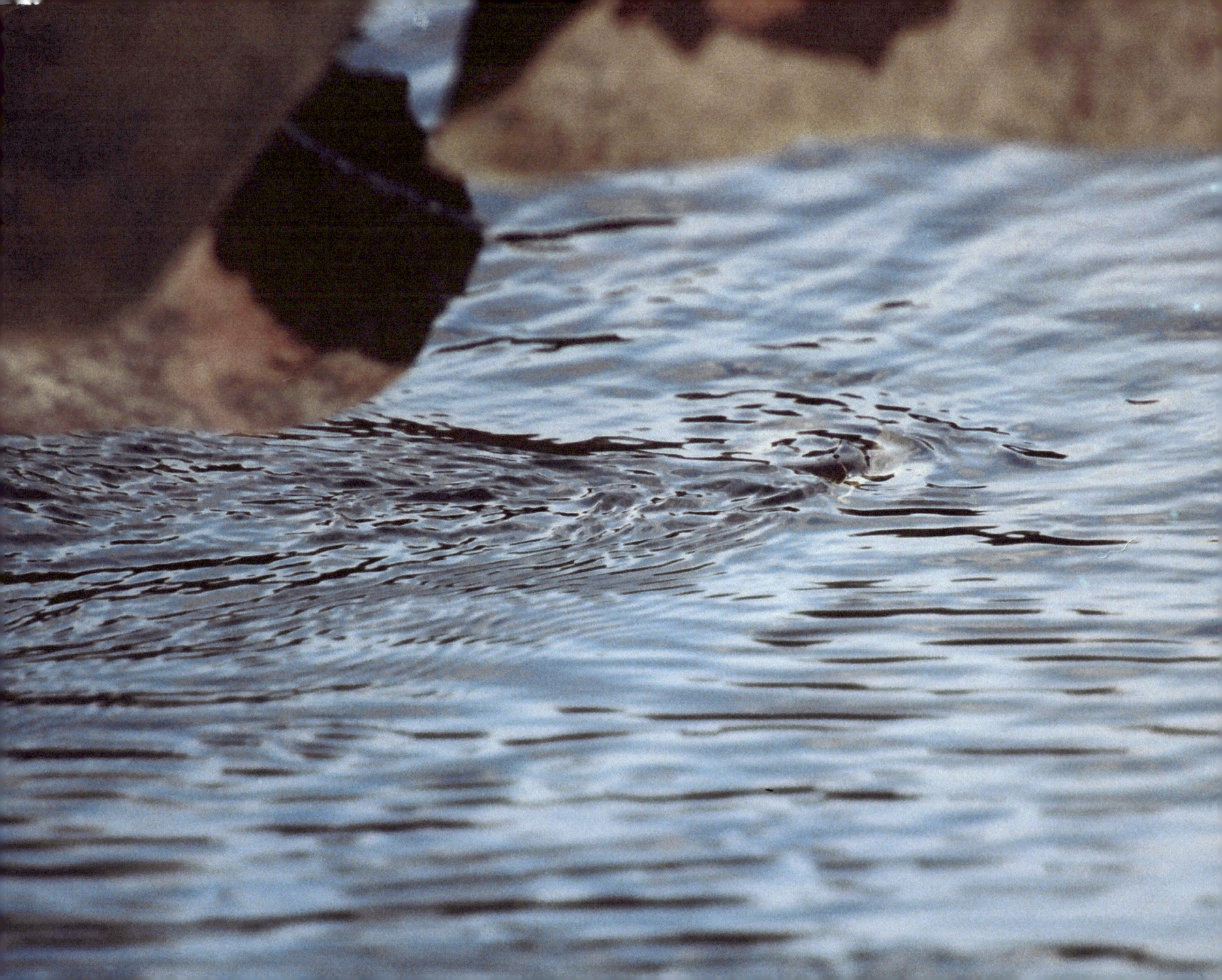

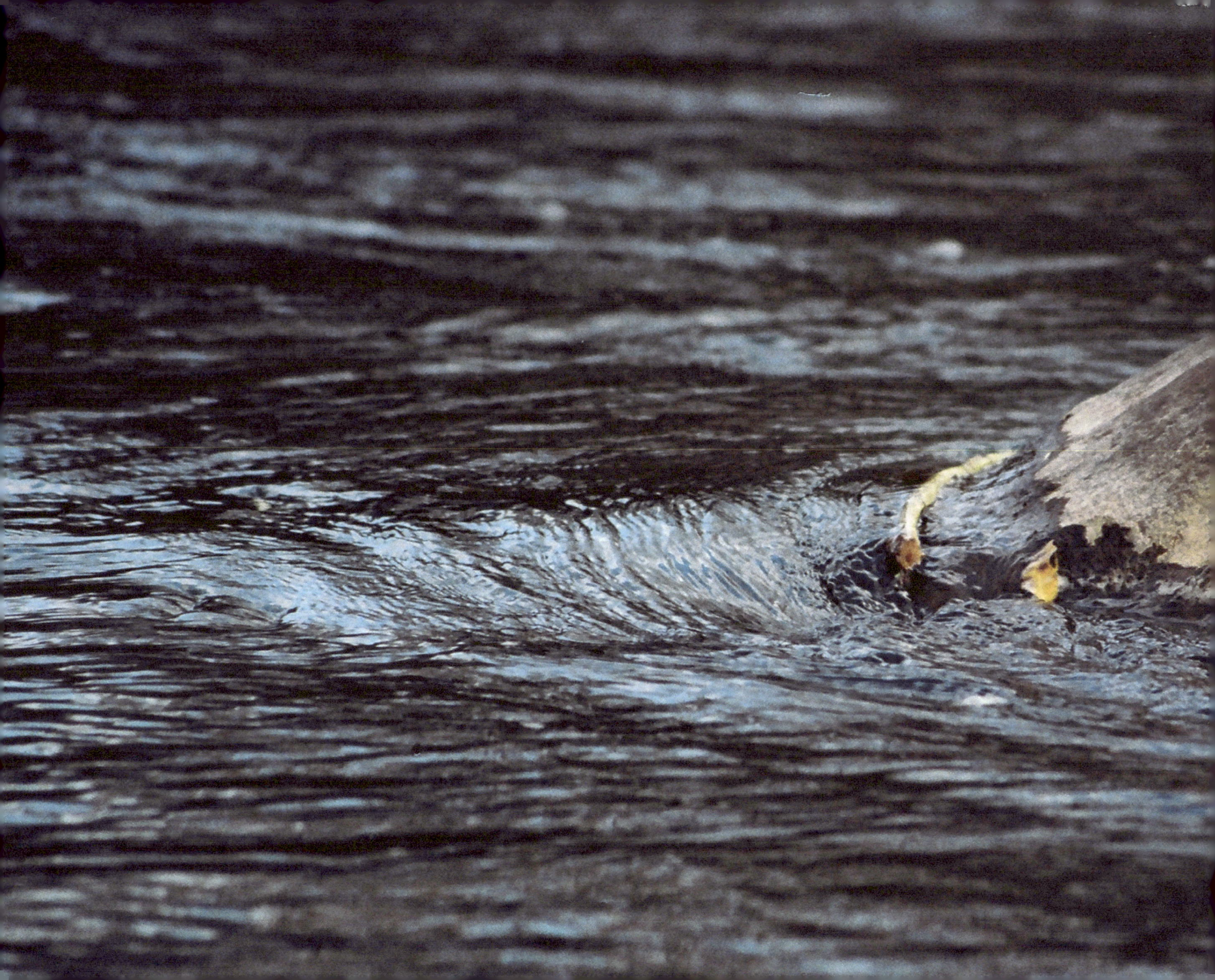

the golden years

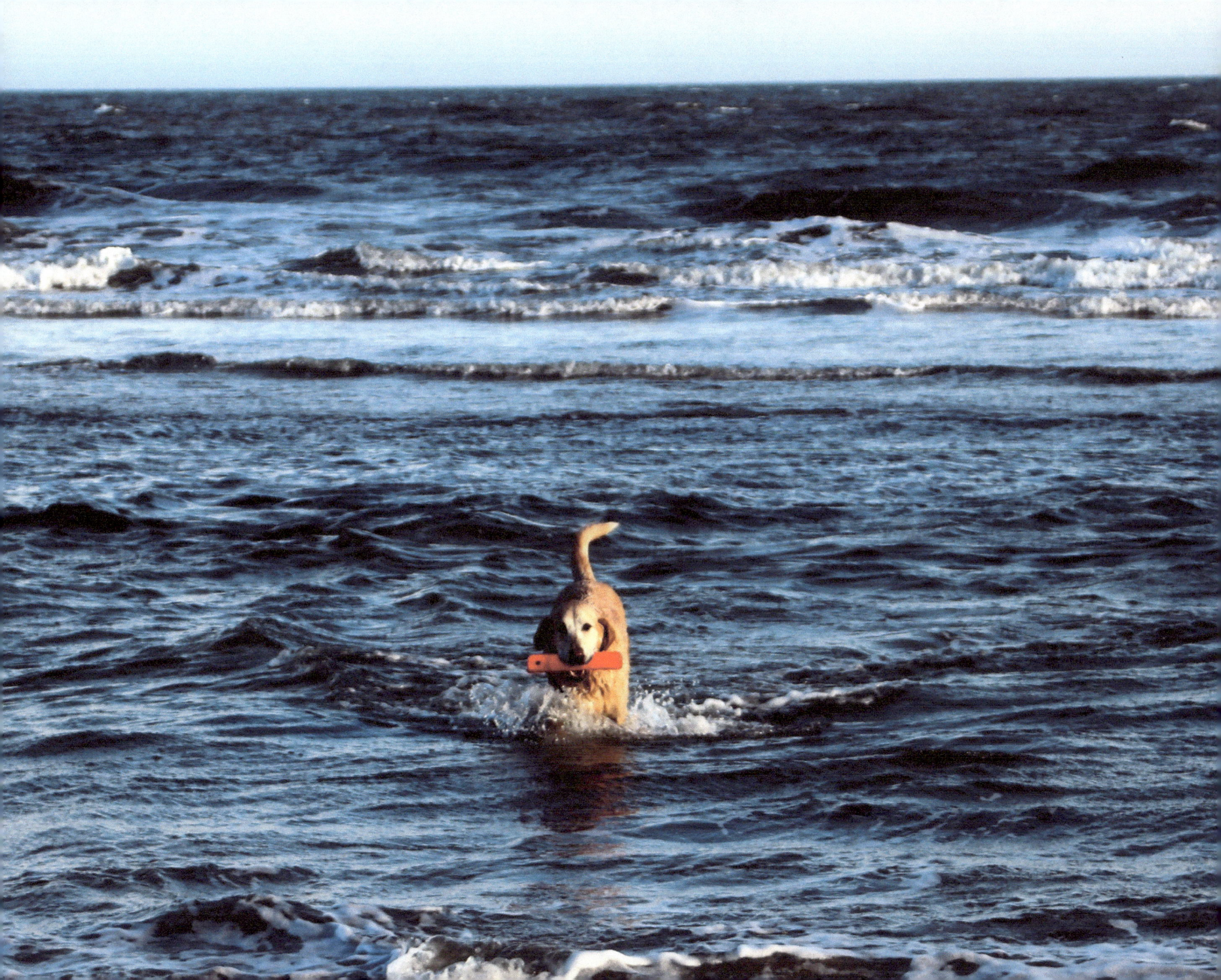

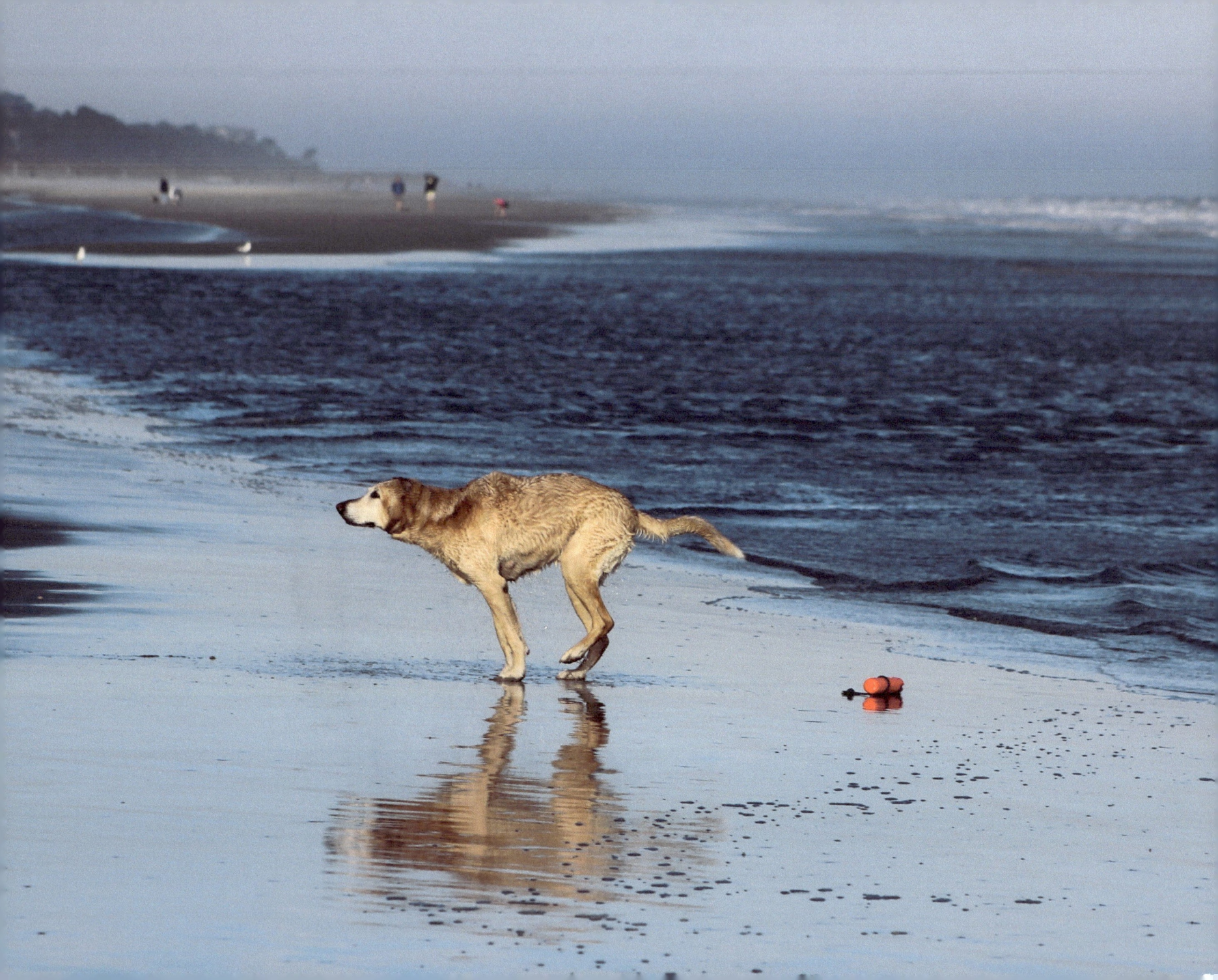

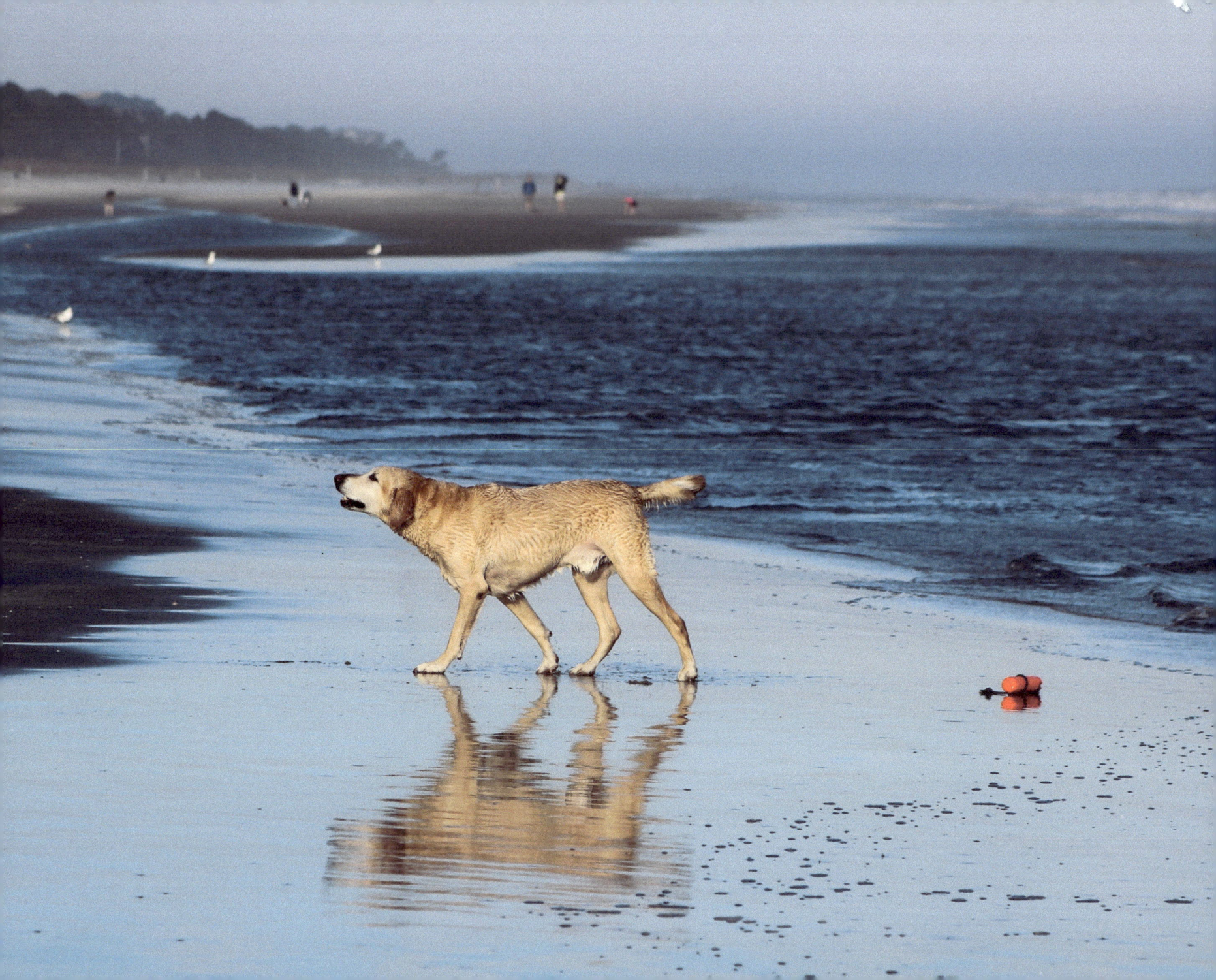

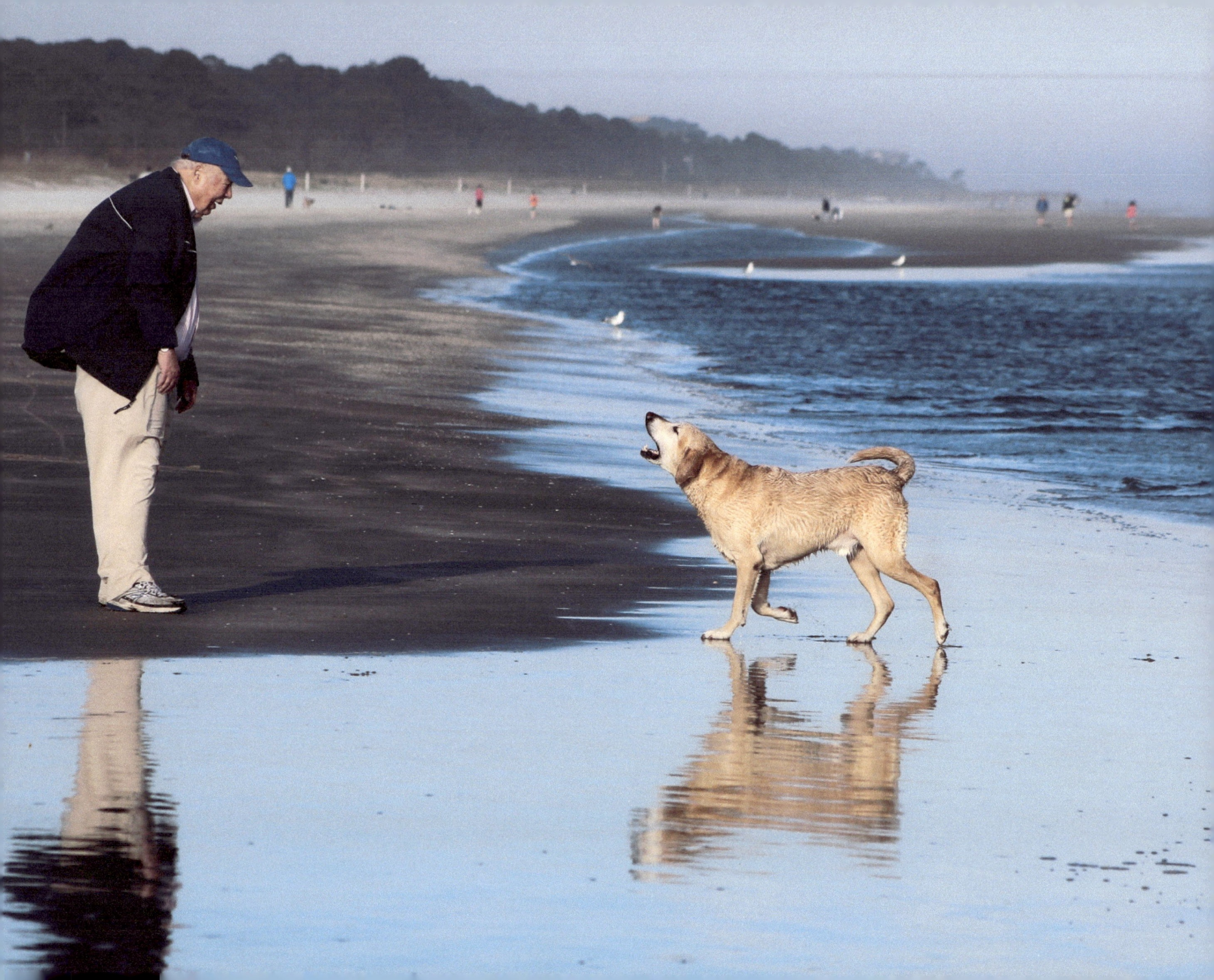

the left coast

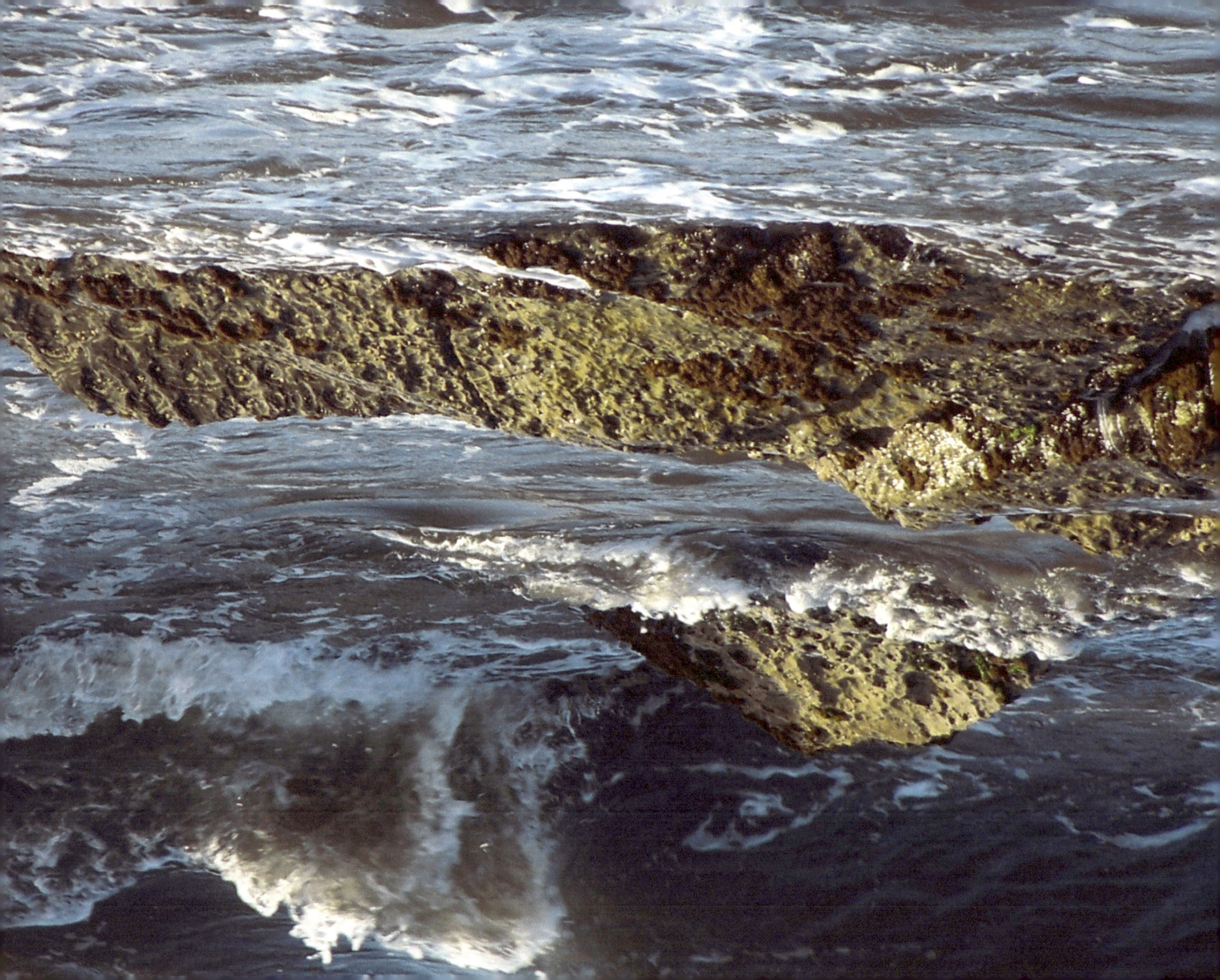

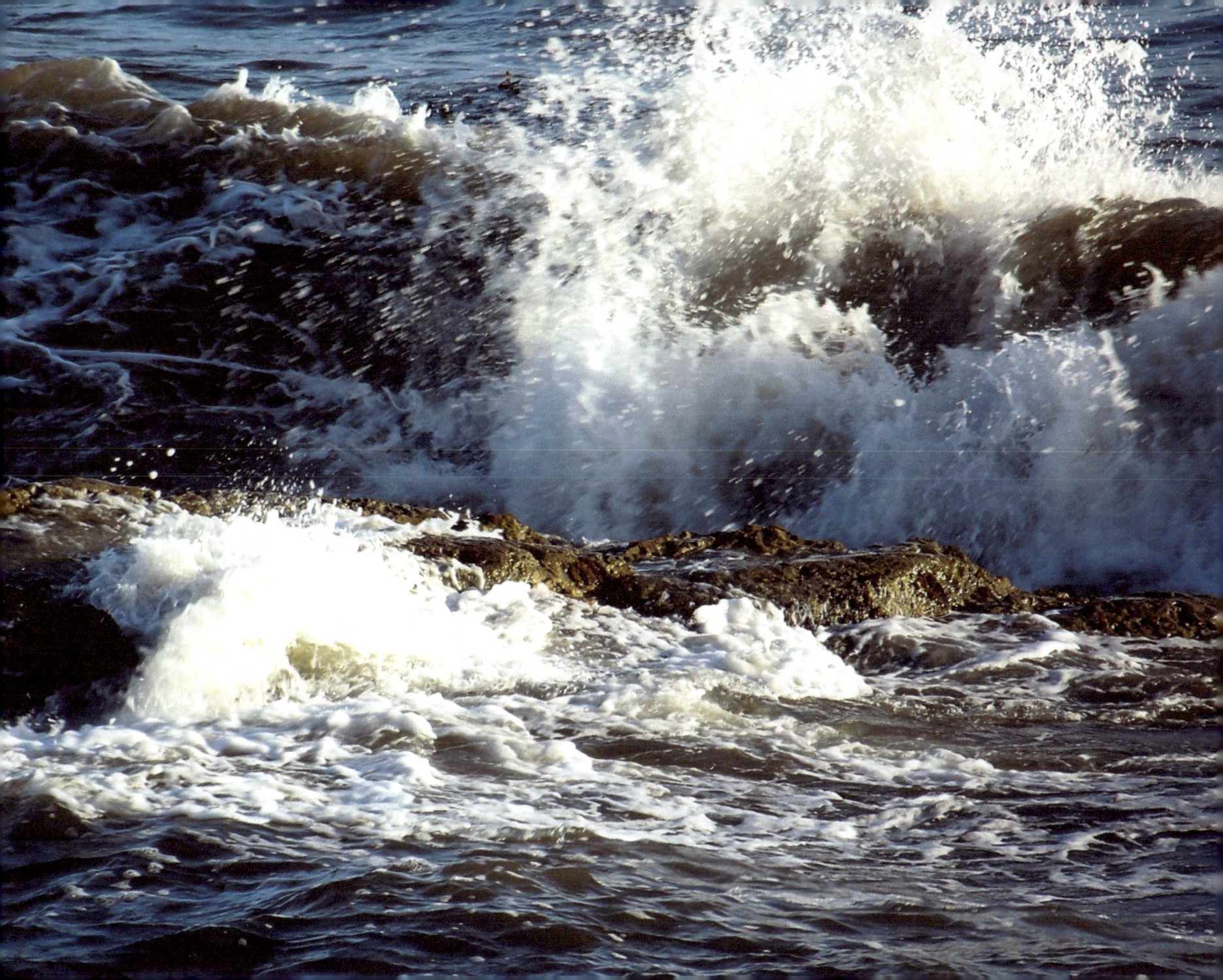

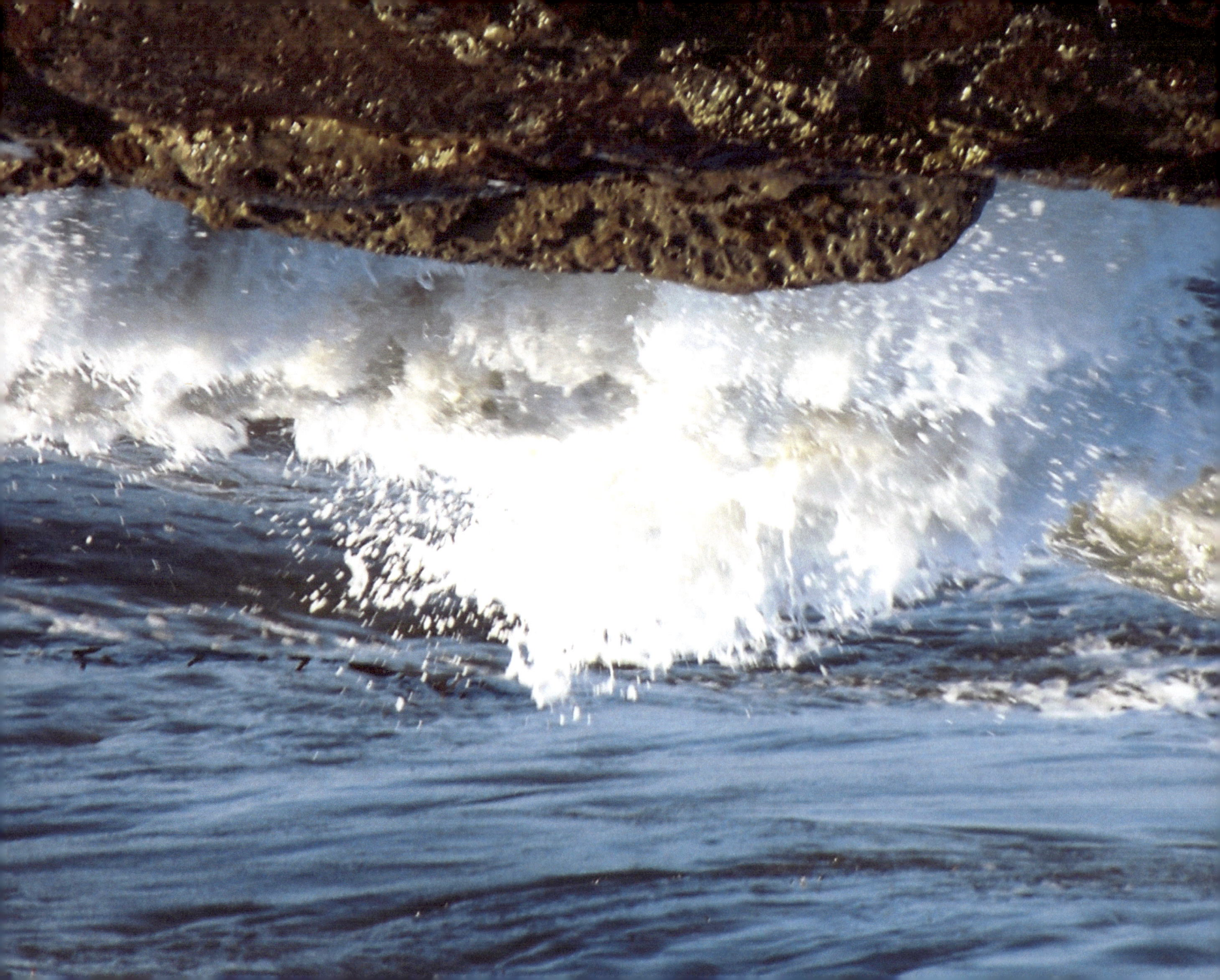

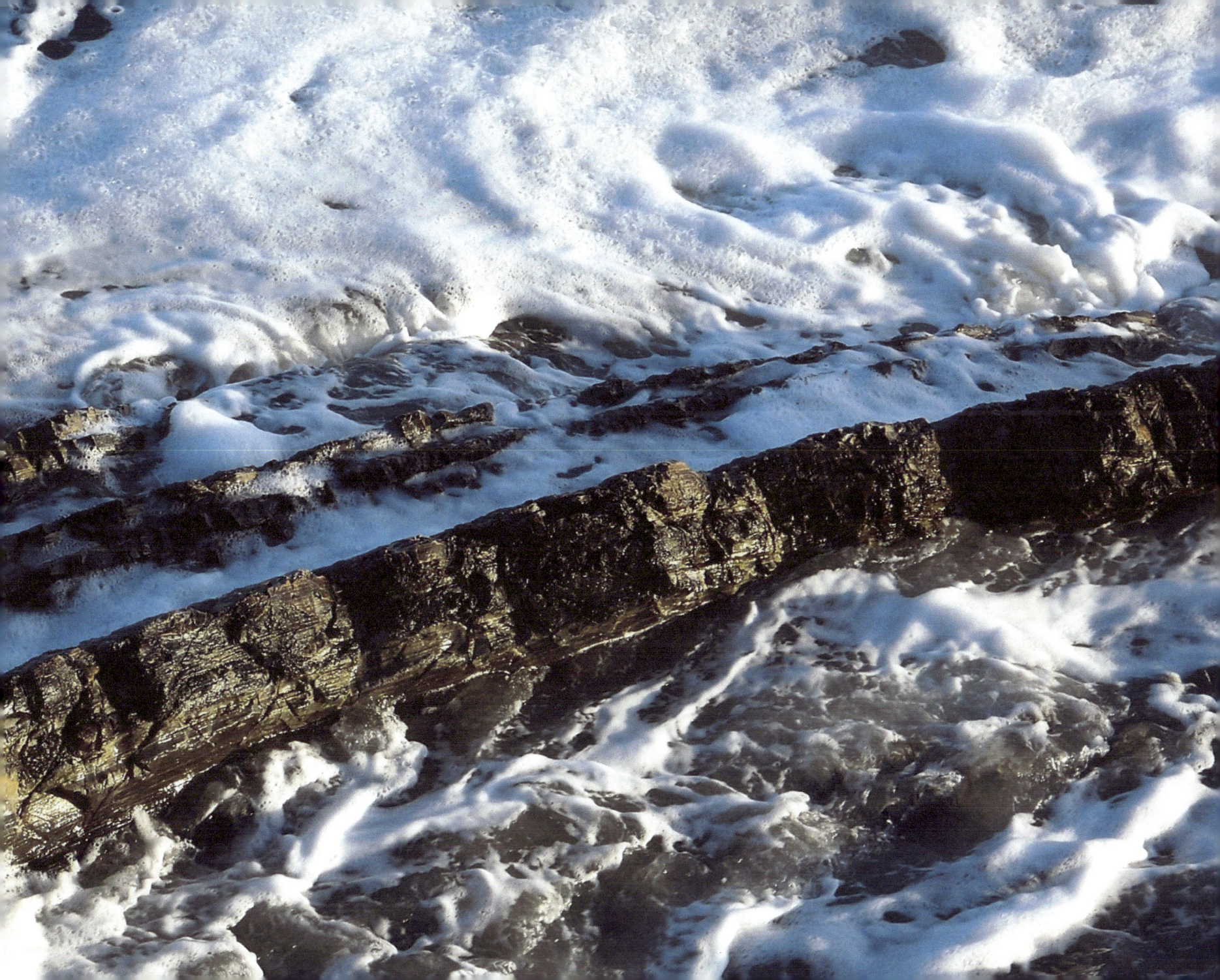

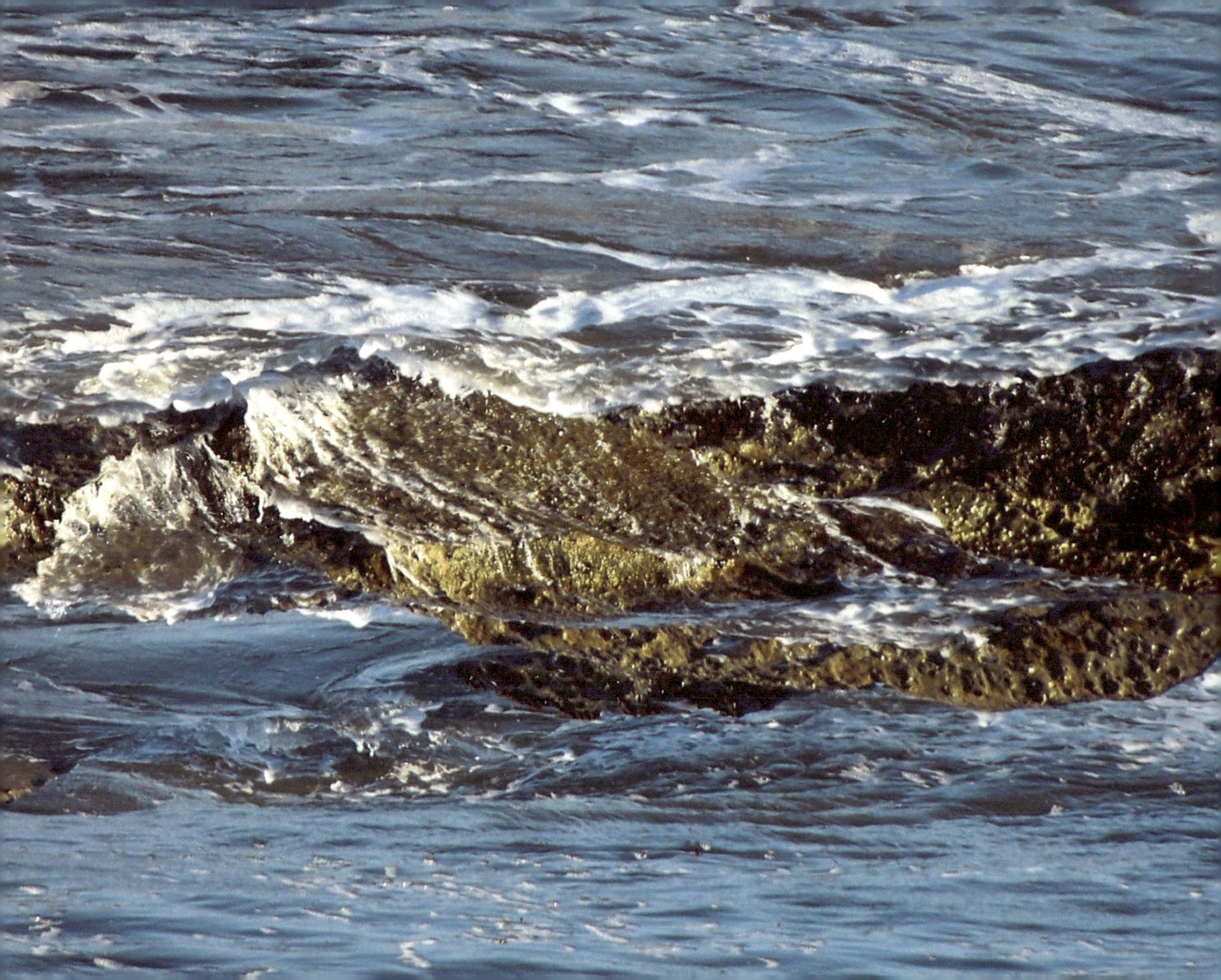

the right side

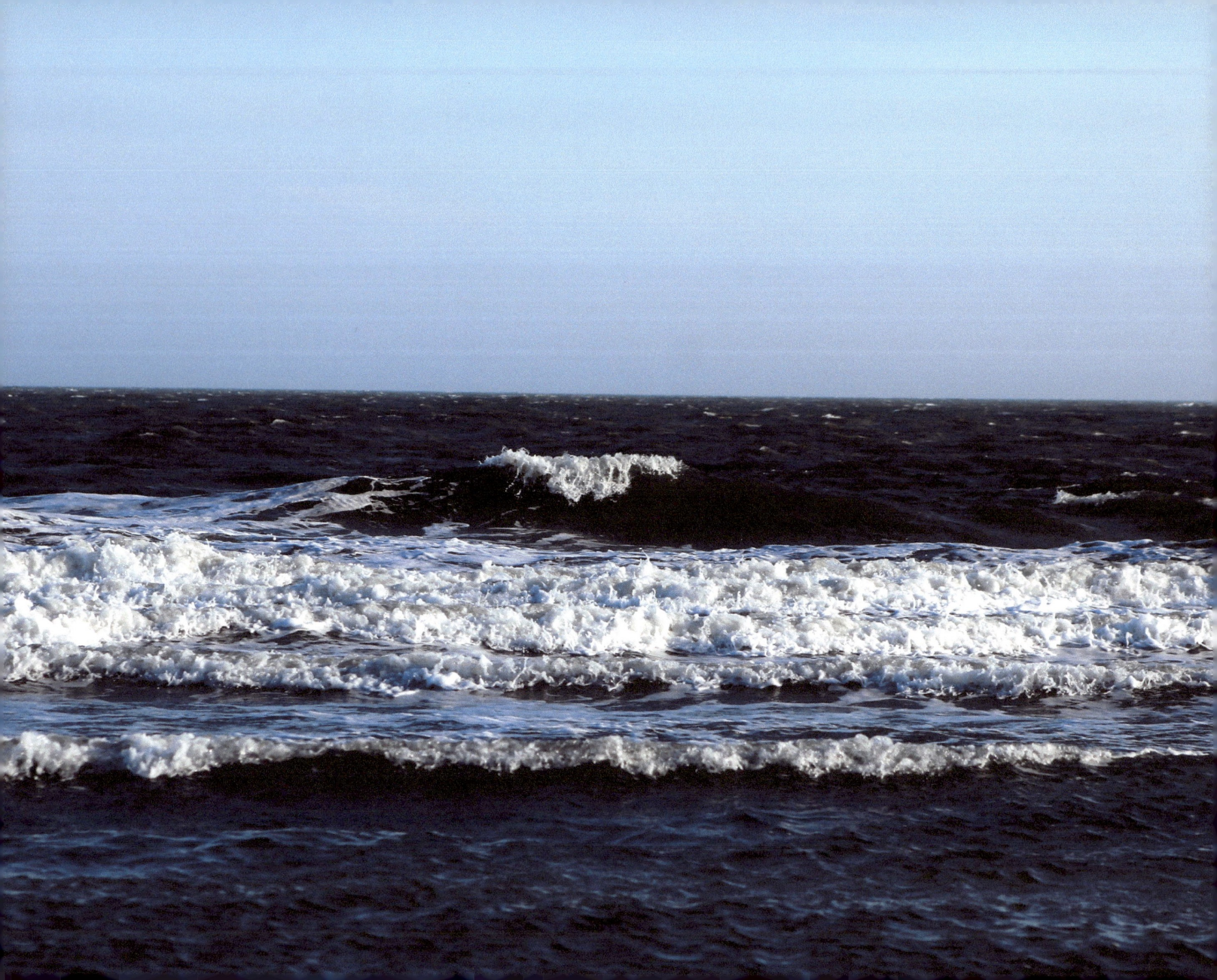

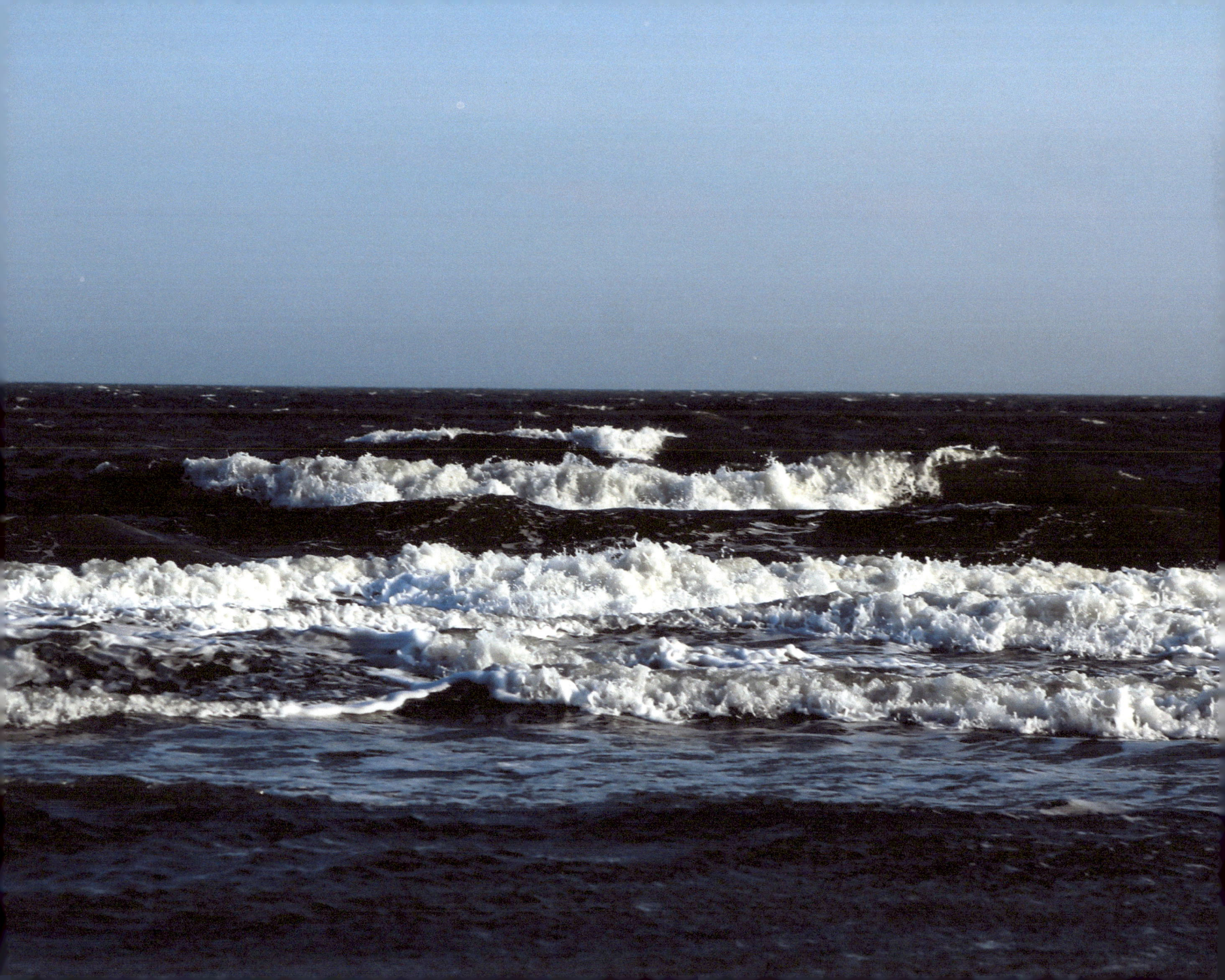

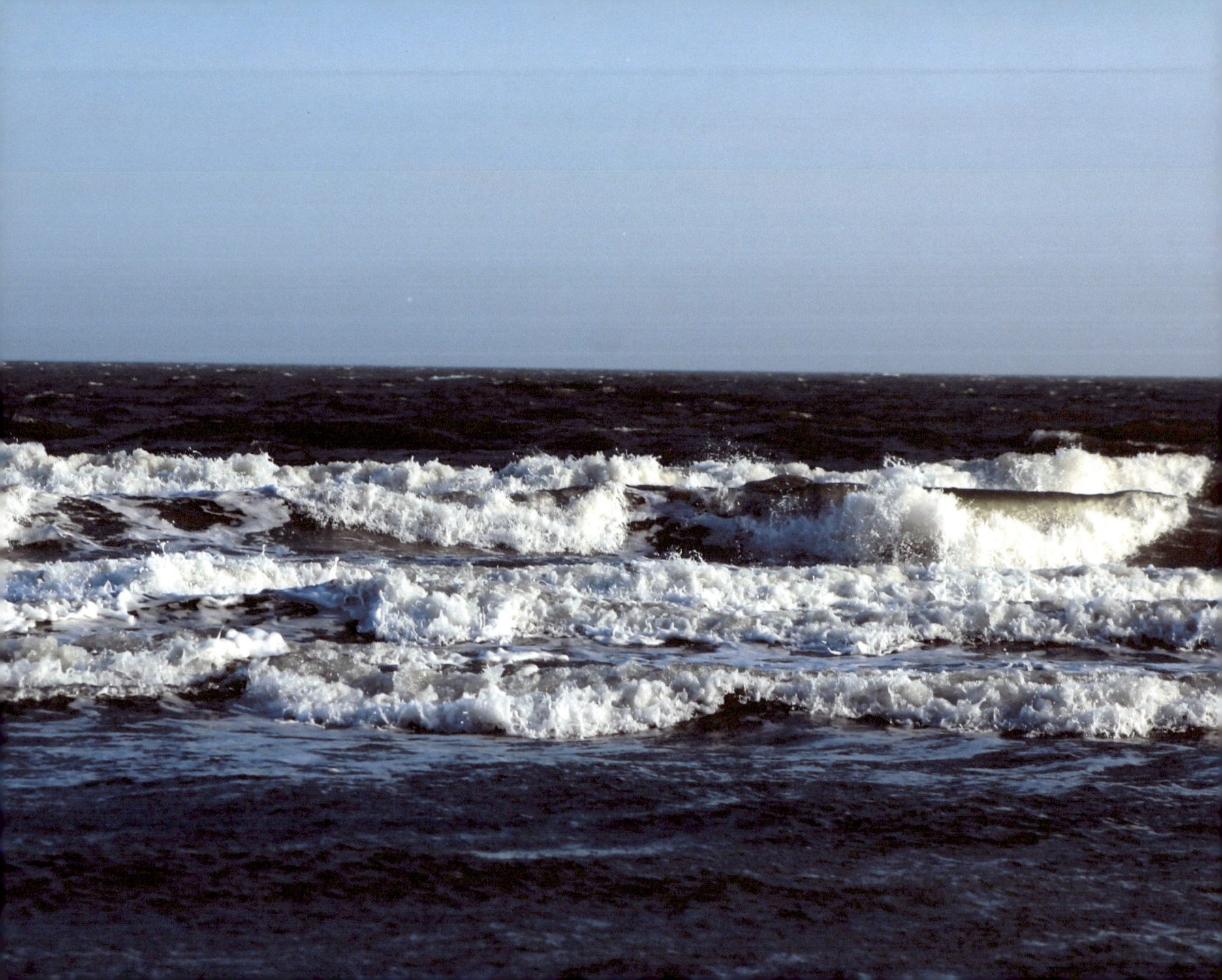

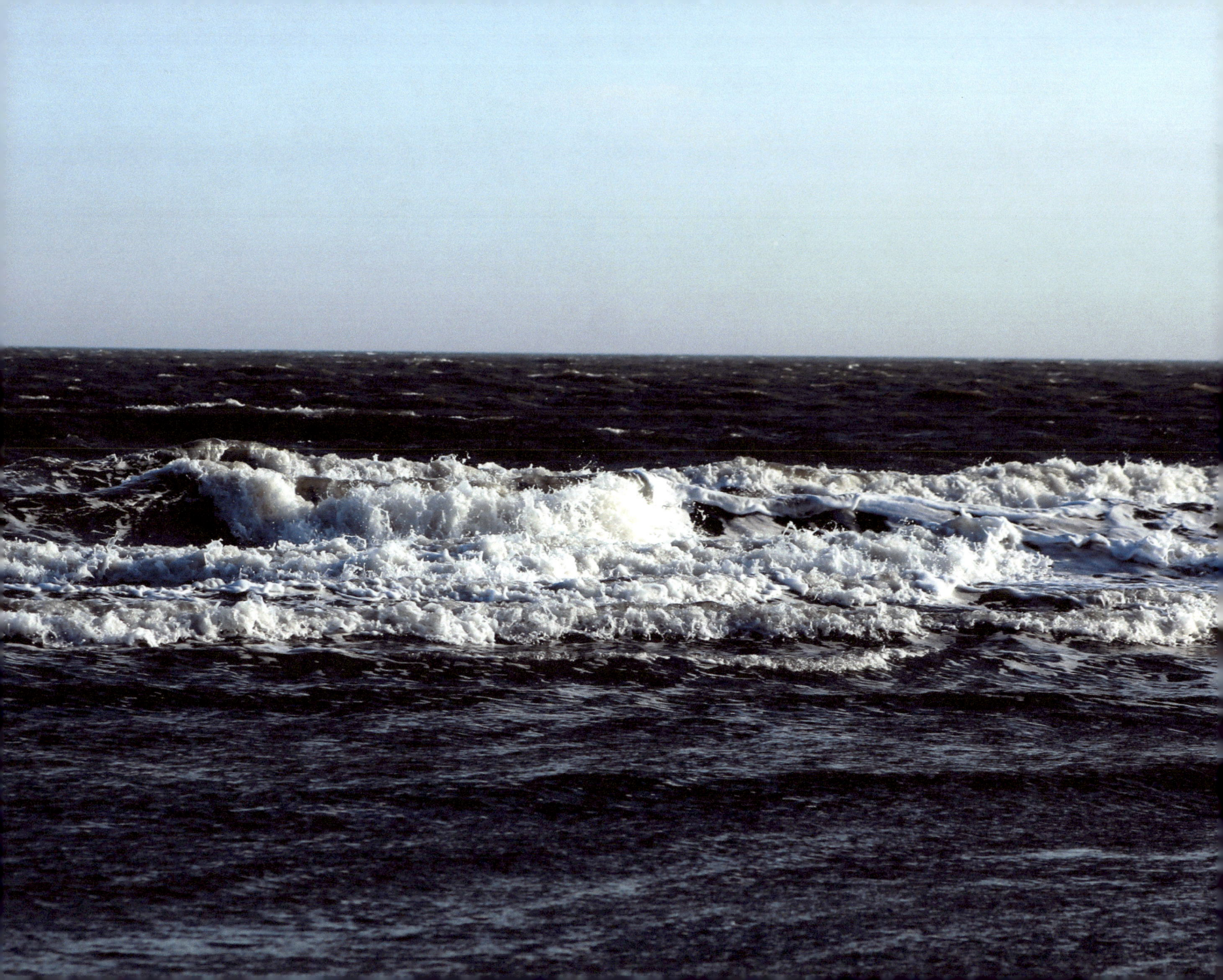

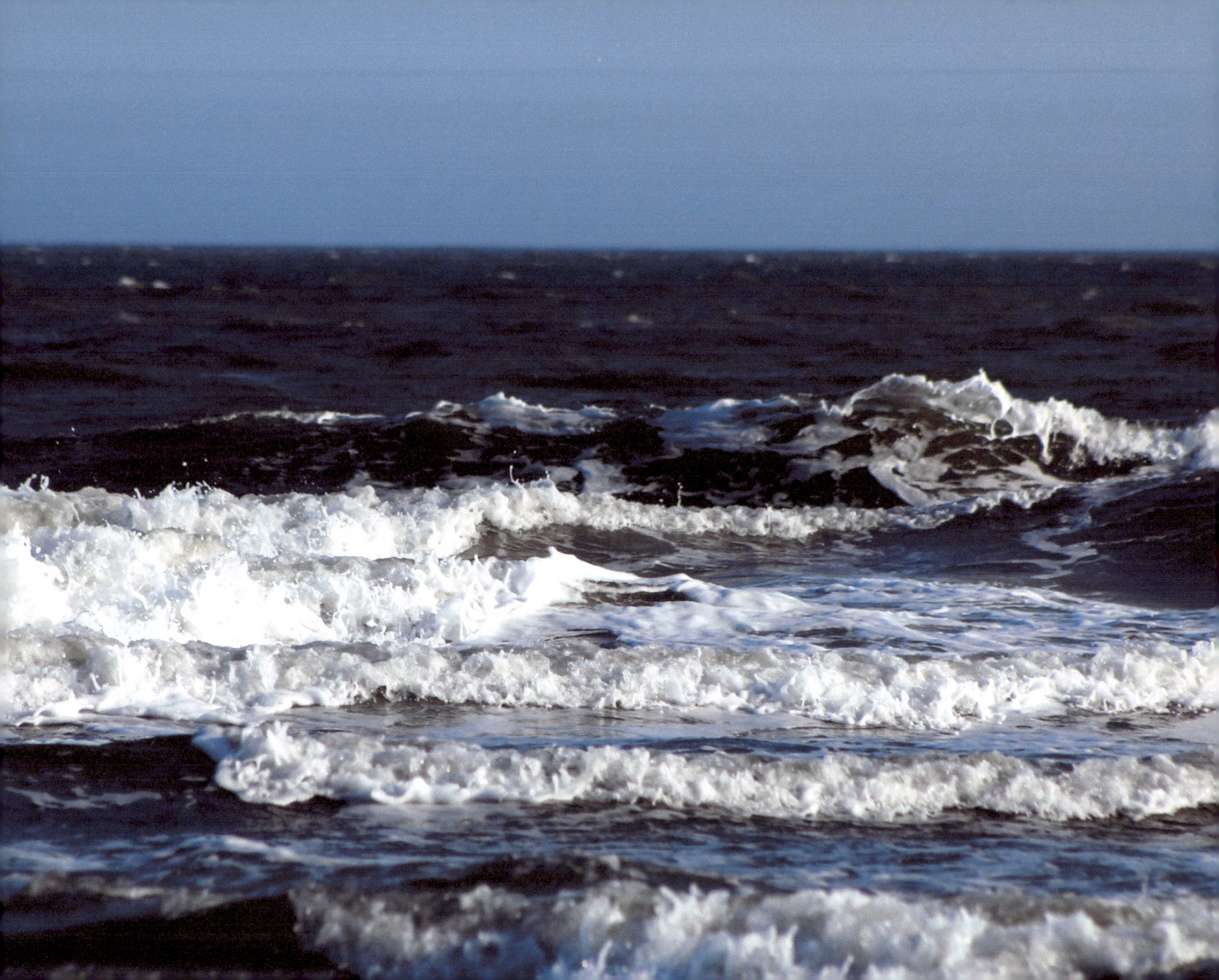

Fox Lullaby

Sleep now cub go to sleep
Sleep now cub I'm here to watch
Stop playing games
Stop chasing tails
Sleep now cub go to sleep
Sleep now cub it's time to sleep
Time to dream
Time to fly
Sleep now cub go to sleep

www.ingramcontent.com/pod-product-compliance
Lightning Source LLC
Chambersburg PA
CBHW040743200526
45159CB00023B/1636